Wordpress Website

Everything You Need to Know to Get Started

(The Complete Guide to Building Websites Using Elementor Page Builder)

Jeffrey Malloy

Published By **Cathy Nedrow**

Jeffrey Malloy

Wordpress Website: Everything You Need to Know to Get Started (The Complete Guide to Building Websites Using Elementor Page Builder)

ISBN 978-1-7772636-9-0

Legal & Disclaimer

The information contained in this book is not designed to replace or take the place of any form of medicine or professional medical advice. The information in this book has been provided for educational & entertainment purposes only.

The information contained in this book has been compiled from sources deemed reliable, and it is accurate to the best of the Author's knowledge; however, the Author cannot guarantee its accuracy and validity and cannot be held liable for any errors or omissions. Changes are periodically made to this book. You must consult your doctor or get professional medical advice before using any of the suggested remedies, techniques, or information in this book.

Table Of Contents

Chapter 1: Setting Up Your Word Press Site

Before you could start developing and coping with your website with Word Press, you need to set up your Word Press internet web page. This includes selecting a website name and web hosting provider, installing Word Press, and configuring a few important settings. In this monetary wreck, we are able to guide you thru those steps and assist you get your Word Press net web page on line up and strolling.

2.1 Choosing a Domain Name and Hosting

Your internet page's net cope with, in conjunction with yourdomain.Com, is known as a internet site call. The enterprise that gives your internet site the room and electricity it dreams on a web server—a computer that links your internet site to the net—is called an internet net web hosting issuer. Selecting an internet website hosting business enterprise and area name is essential as they've an impact on the functionality, protection, and dependability of your internet web page.

When choosing a website name and website hosting issuer, there are several things to keep in thoughts, which consist of:

Availability: Make certain the region call you need to register is loose and hasn't previously been used by someone else. To look for and be a part of up your vicinity call, you may make use of a registrar like Go Daddy or Name cheap. A domain call extension, along side.Com,.Internet, or.Org, is also required and serves to choose out the type of internet website online you are running. You ought to observe and pick the extraordinary extension to your internet site whilst you recollect that a few may additionally have severa prices or specifications.

Brandability: A memorable, catchy area call that is pertinent to the situation rely or sturdy factor of your internet site is important. You need your area name to be precise, carry the man or woman and region of understanding of your internet site, and stand happy with the opposition. Your region name need to not encompass hyphens, numerals, or misspellings due to the truth they may confuse or lie to website site visitors. Additionally, due to the fact a short, honest domain name is straightforward to install writing and recollect, you have to try to keep it that way.

Cost: Keep in mind the price of every web hosting and vicinity call registration and renewal. Depending on the issuer, plan, and offerings you pick out, the rate also can exchange. It is simply helpful to weigh your alternatives and search for offers or reductions that meet your necessities and monetary constraints. It is essential that you be cognizant of any extra charges or levies that some carriers can observe, together with setup, transfer, and renewal charges.

Quality: You ought to pick a website call and net web hosting issuer that offers dependable and tremendous services. You want your internet site to be safe, have little downtime, and cargo fast. A agency organisation with excellent ratings, customer service, and a robust reputation is what you ought to look for. Additionally, you want to evaluation the abilties and specifications that the supplier offers, which include bandwidth, speed, safety, backup, and aid, similarly to garage capacity and tempo.

One of the most critical steps in installing place your WordPress net website on line is deciding on a internet site name and internet hosting provider. Before making your very last desire, you need to evaluate and do a little studies given that it'll have an effect on the improvement and success of your net internet site online.

2.2 Installing WordPress

It is essential to put in WordPress to your internet server after selecting, registering, and internet website hosting your location name. There are number one methods to put in WordPress: mechanically and manually.

Using a website hosting manipulate panel like cPanel or Plesk, create a database and purchaser for WordPress, add the software application software program for your net server using an FTP consumer (together with FileZilla) or Cyberduck, and run the WordPress set up script thru going to https://yourdomain.Com/wp-admin/set up.Personal home internet page. This is the manual set up approach.

Using a software program installer that your web hosting employer gives, such Softaculous or Fantastico, for automatic installation consists of installing WordPress with some clicks and no technical information. All you want to do is get right of access on your internet web hosting control panel, find out the WordPress installer, input your login credentials, website online name, password, and e-mail address, and then pick out out the installation alternative.

WordPress may be installation fast and effects using any approach, even though automated installation is generally advocated for novices because of the reality it's far more on hand. But, a manual installation lets in you greater freedom and manage over your WordPress setup, which includes the capability to select out the WordPress language, model, and region.

It pleasant takes a couple of minutes to put in WordPress, and it's miles a simply easy technique. You may also moreover start building and retaining your internet web site as speedy as WordPress is hooked up with the aid of the usage of logging into your WordPress dashboard.

2.3 Configuring Basic Settings

You need to installation some essential internet website settings after installing WordPress, such the URL, language, time region, date layout, permalinks, and place call. These options, which you could regulate at any 2d from the WordPress dashboard, have an effect on the overall layout and operation of your internet net page.

The following strategies need to be accompanied as a way to set up the essential settings in your internet web web site:

1. Enter your username and password to get proper of access on your WordPress dashboard with the useful resource of going to https://yourdomain.Com/wp-admin/ In your browser.

2. Navigate to Settings > General from the WordPress dashboard's left sidebar menu.

3. Fill up the respective regions with the call of your internet site and tagline. Your internet site's call is its net web site title, and a short declaration or slogan that sums up your internet net page is its tagline. These appear in the browser tab, are seeking engine results, and the header of your internet site.

four. In the relevant sections, enter the deal with of your WordPress net website online on line and WordPress cope with. Your internet site on line cope with is the URL of your net website online, whilst your WordPress address is the URL of your WordPress set up. Unless you have got WordPress mounted in a subfolder or subdomain of your internet website online, they are regularly the equal. Your WordPress URL might be https://yourdomain.Com/weblog, at the equal time as your internet site deal with can be https://yourdomain.Com, for example, if WordPress was hooked up in a subdirectory named weblog.

five. From the drop-down menu, choose out the language of your internet website. The language used by your WordPress dashboard and net website on line is called your website on line language. WordPress allows masses of languages; you can installation more languages with the aid of the use of navigating to the Site Language segment within the Updates show of your WordPress admin.

6. Select it slow zone the usage of the choice that drops under. The time vicinity that your WordPress dashboard and net web site

are in is similar to your personal. Alternatively, you can appoint the UTC (Coordinated Universal Time) choice and enter the offset from UTC in hours, or you can pick out from a list of cities or regions that correspond in your time area.

7. You can also furthermore input your non-public custom formats or choose out your selected date and time codecs from the drop-down boxes. Your WordPress dashboard and net web web page display dates and times the use of your date format and time layout. The PHP date and time layout characters can be used to acquire custom formats, or you could pick out from a number of favored forms. As an example, F j, Y could possibly show November 23, 2023 because of the truth the date, while g:i a must show 10:forty six am as the time.

8. Select the selection "Your Week Starts" from the drop-down menu. The day that your WordPress dashboard and internet site make use of due to the fact the primary day of the

week is the choice that determines at the same time as your week starts. Sunday through Saturday are your options, based totally on non-public flavor or cultural norms.

9. To maintain your options, click on on the Save Changes button positioned at the bottom of the display screen.

Setting up the crucial settings to your Word Press internet web site is a crucial first step. In accordance with the goal and goal market of your net website on-line, you have got to test and modify those parameters. Other Word Press dashboard options, such those for writing, studying, discussions, media, and privateness, are also open for exploration and change.

Chapter 2: Exploring Word Press Themes

One of the most thrilling and important factors of making and dealing with your website with Word Press is deciding on and customizing your challenge. A subject matter is a fixed of files that outline the format, format, and fashion of your internet net page. A subject rely should have an effect on the appearance and capability of your internet web page, in addition to the client experience and feature an impact on of your web page visitors. In this bankruptcy, we're capable of find out WordPress topics and show you the way to pick out out, installation, and personalize your mission.

three.1 Introduction to WordPress Themes

The template hierarchy precept, on which WordPress subjects are built, states that diverse content sorts are displayed on your net website by using the usage of WordPress using tremendous templates. WordPress, for instance, shows your homepage the usage of the index.Php template, a unmarried post using the single.Personal home page template, a single net web page the usage of the internet net web page.Personal domestic page template, and so on. The WordPress Codex has the entire list of templates alongside their hierarchy.

WordPress problems similarly make use of template tags, which can be PHP strategies that show or achieve data from your net website, much like the name of the net web page, posts, content material cloth, dates, authors, and so on. The whole listing of template tags and the way to use them is to be had within the WordPress Codex.

Style sheets are documents that embody CSS (Cascading Style Sheets) code that manages the appearance and formatting of your website, which includes sun shades, fonts, margins, padding, borders, and so on. These files also are utilized by WordPress topics. A WordPress problem depend's number one fashion sheet is regularly named `style.Css` and consists of statistics about the concern rely, like its call, description, version, writer, and license. The whole series of style sheet values and attributes is to be had inside the [W3Schools].

WordPress problems moreover rent scripts, which might be documents with JavaScript code that decorate your net web site's capability and interplay with elements like menus, sliders, animations, transitions, and results. The code that specifies a WordPress situation rely's capabilities and selections, such its menus, widgets, customizer, and extraordinary elements, is frequently positioned inside the primary script, `functions.Php`. The complete set of script sports and additives is available inside the W3Schools.

WordPress issues might also additionally rent photographs, which might be documents with graphical components like headers, backgrounds, emblems, and icons that decorate the appearance and experience of your internet web web page. A WordPress subject matter's pix are frequently saved in a folder named `pix` in the assignment be counted folder. The technique `get_template_directory_uri()` may be used to get the issue be counted folder's URL.

plugins are bits of code that improve or upload new capability to WordPress troubles. Examples of these capabilities consist of social media buttons, e-change gear, contact office work, and extra. Plugins can be used with subject matters the use of hooks, filters, and shortcodes, and may be installed and enabled via the WordPress dashboard. The entire list of plugins and their functionalities is available in the WordPress Plugin Directory.

3.2 Choosing and Installing a Theme

Depending on the purpose, audience, and fashion of your net web site, deciding on a topic is an person and subjective desire. Nonetheless, there are a few established necessities thru which you can determine and evaluation severa topics, which incorporates:

Functionality: A subject matter should include all of the functions and customizations you want on your net web website online, including layout, navigation, compatibility, responsiveness, and accessibility. Additionally, you want to evaluate the concern rely's safety and functionality, which consist of its replace frequency, seo optimization, code excellent, and loading tempo.

Design: You should pick out out a topic that enhances the colours, fonts, pictures, icons, and everyday fashion you want for your internet net page. It is sincerely useful to examine the difficulty count number's degree of customization and versatility, which consist of its functionality to modify settings, encompass custom CSS and little one topics, and upload your very non-public material.

Assistance: You should pick a subject that gives reliable and beneficial assistance through e mail, forums, tutorials, and documentation. Along with the issue rely's ratings and critiques, you should moreover undergo customer comments and endorsements.

You may additionally additionally select out from hundreds of WordPress issues which might be available for gratis or buy. Go to Appearance > Themes > Add New inside the WordPress dashboard to find out and installation subjects. By heading to Appearance > Themes > Add New > Upload Theme, you can additionally download problem subjects from unique net web sites, such WordPress.Org Themes Directory, ThemeForest, or Elegant Themes, and upload them on your WordPress dashboard.

The following techniques ought to be observed in case you need to installation a subject from the WordPress dashboard:

1. Open your browser, visit `https://yourdomain.Com/wp-admin/, and enter your username and password to get proper of access on your WordPress dashboard.

2. In the WordPress dashboard's left sidebar menu, choose Appearance > Themes > Add New.

3. Either browse or use the filters, classes, tags, or key phrases to look for the challenge count you want to put in. Additionally, you could click on on the Preview button to get a preview of the subject, or you can click on at the Theme records link to appearance extra statistics.

4. To exercise the situation rely in your internet internet web page, click on on at the Install button. A Installing Theme observe and a development bar indicating the set up kingdom can be established to you.

five. Press the Activate button to make your net site's situation count energetic. A Theme activated notification and a Customize link will appear to you.

It's easy and a laugh to select out and deploy a subject depend for your internet site, which lets you make brief changes to the manner it seems and works. By heading to Appearance > Themes and choosing the Activate button of the preferred situation, you can furthermore exchange topics at any 2nd.

3.Three Customizing Your Theme

You can also extraordinary-music and customize your internet net page to fit your requirements and tastes via manner of customizing your challenge remember, this is an interesting and innovative machine. The WordPress customizer is a stay preview device that lets in you to appearance adjustments you're making for your net website in real time, and it may be used to customise your challenge. Using child subjects and custom CSS, greater state-of-the-art techniques that can help you alter your situation depend's code without changing the primary trouble, you may in addition customize it.

You must do the following movements so that you can adjust your problem count the use of the WordPress customizer:

1. Open your browser, visit `https://yourdomain.Com/wp-admin/, and input your username and password to get entry to your WordPress dashboard.

2. Click the Customize hyperlink inside the Themes show or the Toolbar on the top of your net site, or visit Appearance > Customize inside the WordPress dashboard's left sidebar menu.

3. Examine and adjust the challenge depend number's available settings and options, which includes the homepage settings, colours, fonts, header, history, menus, and widgets. The preview panel at the proper thing of the show display suggests the modifications you're making in your net web page.

4. Press the Publish button placed at the top of the internet page to save and activate your internet site changes. Additionally, you have had been given the selection to preserve your changes without publishing them thru clicking the Save Draft button or to undo your

adjustments and bypass back to the initial settings thru clicking the Discard Changes button.

You may additionally moreover exhibit your creativity and feel of favor in your internet site with the resource of the usage of without problem and joyfully personalizing the topic on your internet site. Additionally, you may take a look at and take a look at numerous configurations and capabilities till you determine something works great to your website.

Chapter 3: Mastering Word Press Plugging

Plugins are one of the most effective and useful capabilities of WordPress, as they will let you add new features or beautify contemporary-day ones for your internet web page. Plugins are portions of code that interact with WordPress and your problem, and they may be capable of perform severa skills, which includes including touch bureaucracy, social media buttons, e-trade equipment, and so on. In this financial disaster, we're capable of offer an reason for what plugins are, a manner to choose out out and installation them, and the manner to configure and control them.

four.1 What Are Plugins?

Essentially, plugins are accessories or extensions that change or enhance WordPress's and your state of affairs's skills. Plugins can be uploaded manually or set up and enabled via the WordPress dashboard. They can be made via the usage of you, thru special developers, or thru way of WordPress developers. The WordPress dashboard moreover lets in for the updating, deactivation, and deletion of plugins.

Hooks, filters, and shortcodes are techniques through which plugins speak with WordPress and your topic. WordPress hooks are places wherein you could add your non-public code or capability. Examples of hooks include the loading of WordPress, the e-book of a publish, and the submission of a statement. The content material cloth of a publish, the pick out of a web page, or the URL of a link may all be changed or changed the use of filters in WordPress or your difficulty. Shortcodes are HTML codes that you could insert into your posts or pages to reveal or run a plugin's function, this sort of video, gallery, or contact form.

Depending on their use and cause, plugins may be divided into numerous classes, collectively with:

Security plugins: These are plugins that provide skills like firewall, antivirus, backup, or captcha to defend your net web website online from dangers like unsolicited mail, malware, hackers, and extraordinary on line criminal interest.

Performance plugins: These are plugins that add competencies like caching, compression, minification, or lazy loading for your internet internet site to increase its standard normal performance and overall overall performance.

search engine marketing plugins: These are plugins that upload abilities like analytics, sitemaps, meta tags, and breadcrumbs on your website to make it more are looking for for engine friendly.

Social plugins: These are plugins that upload functionality like feeds, remarks, sharing buttons, and check buttons to your internet site at the way to be part of it with social media networks.

E-trade plugins: These are plugins that upload capability like a buying cart, checkout, price processor, or inventory to allow you to sell gadgets or offerings on your net web web page.

Contact plugins: By together with abilities like touch paperwork, e-mail marketing and advertising, stay chat, or assist tickets, these plugins can help you have interaction along with your internet site's internet site visitors or clients.

Media plugins: These are plugins that add functionality like galleries, sliders, lightboxes, or game enthusiasts to beautify how media belongings are displayed and controlled for your internet website online.

Editor plugins: These are accessories to your internet net page that decorate editing and writing thru introducing capabilities like blocks, widgets, shortcodes, or templates.

Since plugins offer many options and answers on your internet web page's requirements and desires, they will be crucial for the use of WordPress to create and hold a a achievement, commercial organization-like internet site. Plugins do, however, include numerous dangers and downsides, collectively with:

Compatibility: Plugins couldn't paintings collectively collectively with your subject matter, WordPress version, or one-of-a-kind plugins, which would possibly motive conflicts, troubles, or internet website crashes. Prior to putting in any plugins, you want to continually verify their compatibility and look at client reviews. You should additionally test any new functions on a neighborhood or staging server in advance than allowing them to your primary net internet web site.

Quality: The functionality, protection, and usability of your internet site may be impacted via poorly evolved, poorly documented, or poorly maintained plugins. Instead of making use of out-of-date, abandoned, or pirated plugins, you have to constantly use top notch and honest plugins from reliable property similar to the WordPress Plugin Directory, CodeCanyon, or WooCommerce.

Quantity: Plugins also can moreover add capabilities or functionalities on your net web site which may be superfluous or redundant, which could likely purpose your net site to load extra slowly, use more assets, or clog your dashboard. Avoid utilizing many plugins that do the same venture and pleasant employ the plugins you want. Delete any plugins you are not using.

4.2 Essential Plugins for Beginners

The sheer quantity and variety of plugins available might possibly make you feel beaten or confused in case you're new to WordPress and plugins. Based on their nice, usefulness, and reputation, we've got have been given put together a listing of a few want to-have plugins for beginners to get you began. These plugins address protection, typical overall performance, seo, social networking, e-alternate, touch, media, and editor—a number of the maximum critical components of building and keeping a net website. Of direction, you could have severa requirements and tastes on your internet website, so experience unfastened to research and attempt out one in every of a type plugins that in form the feature and aesthetic of your internet web site.

Here are some of the most critical plugins for emblem spanking new users:

1. Jetpack: This plugin gives a number of functions and offerings, together with backup, protection, performance, format, marketing and marketing, and further, to beautify and defend your net web page. The agency that created WordPress.Com, Automattic, is the only that creates Jetpack, which connects your internet net web page to one-of-a-kind structures like Google, Facebook, and Twitter. Depending on the functions and services you

want, Jetpack offers some of top elegance plans in addition to a unfastened one.

2. Yoast search engine marketing: This plugin offers capabilities like clarity evaluation, sitemaps, breadcrumbs, meta tags, and key-phrase research to help you optimize your internet net site for search engines like google like google and yahoo like google and yahoo. One of the most famous and substantially used search engine marketing plugins is Yoast search engine advertising; it is available in versions: a unfastened version and a industrial corporation model with more functionality and beneficial resource.

three. WooCommerce: With the help of this plugin, you can add abilties for your net internet website, like items, orders, customers, reductions, evaluations, and extra, and run an internet shop. With masses of extensions and issues to choose out from, WooCommerce is the maximum properly-favored and strong e-exchange plugin for

WordPress, allowing you to further personalize and decorate your business enterprise. Although WooCommerce is free to apply, some of its issue subjects and plugins aren't.

four. Contact Form 7: This plugin offers you the functionality to apply a easy and adaptable markup language to assemble and manipulate contact bureaucracy in your net website online. One of the right and most dependable touch shape plugins is Contact Form 7, which additionally consists of some of add-ons and connectors to boom its competencies, such reCAPTCHA, PayPal, and Mailchimp. While Contact Form 7 can be used without fee, many integrations and accessories need rate.

5. Elementor: With the help of this plugin, you could use a drag-and-drop interface to design and regulate lovely, responsive internet sites. You can also accumulate your internet website the usage of a library of templates, widgets, and additives through

way of the usage of Elementor, one of the most nicely-appreciated and effective web page builder plugins. There is a seasoned model of Elementor that provides more features and help, and a unfastened version as well.

four.Three Installing and Configuring Plugins

It honestly takes some clicks to install and configure plugins to your internet website, supplying you with the capability to short add new functions or enhance contemporary ones. By deciding on Plugins > Add New or Plugins > Installed Plugins from the WordPress dashboard, you could set up and customise plugins. Additionally, through heading to Plugins > Add New > Upload Plugin, you could get plugins from different net websites like CodeCanyon, WordPress.Org Plugins Directory, or [WooCommerce and add them on your WordPress dashboard.

The following techniques need to be found in an effort to install and configure a plugin from the WordPress dashboard:

1. Open your browser, visit `https://yourdomain.Com/wp-admin/, and input your username and password to access your WordPress dashboard.

2. From the WordPress dashboard's left sidebar menu, choose Plugins > Add New.

3. Use the filters, training, tags, or key phrases to browse or look for the plugin you want to put in. Additionally, with the aid of selecting the Details & Reviews tab, you could browse more records or preview the plugin by using clicking the More Details link.

4. To installation the plugin for your internet web page, click on at the Install Now button. A improvement bar that indicates the installation united states of the usa could be hooked up, at the side of a notification that reads Installing Plugin.

five. Press Activate to make the plugin energetic in your internet website online. A word pointing out Plugin activated and a link classified Settings or Configure will seem.

6. To get admission to the plugin's settings and alternatives, click on on the Settings or Configure hyperlink, or visit the plugin's menu or phase within the WordPress dashboard. By selecting the Settings or Configure hyperlink beneath the plugin's call, you may additionally get proper of get entry to to the plugin's options and settings via way of heading to Plugins > Installed Plugins.

7. Examine and alter the plugin's settings and parameters according alongside facet your requirements and tastes. By clicking on the Documentation or help link under the plugin's call, or via going to the plugin's website or dialogue board, you can also see the plugin's documentation, tutorials, or assist.

With just a few clicks, you could quick and effects personalize and decorate your net internet site online by the usage of the use of putting in and customizing plugins. By heading to Plugins > Installed Plugins and choosing the Update, Deactivate, or do away with hyperlink below the plugin's name, you may moreover update, deactivate, or take away plugins from the WordPress dashboard.

Creating Compelling Content

Content is the center and essence of your net website online, as it conveys your message, records, or cost to your web website online site visitors and clients. Content may be in the shape of textual content, pics, audio, video, or particular media, and it may be used for numerous capabilities, such as informing, training, interesting, or persuading your audience. Creating compelling content material is a key functionality and venture for any internet net website proprietor, as it calls for creativity, readability, and consistency. In this monetary disaster, we will display you the way to create and manage your content material using the WordPress editor, and a manner to feature and layout text and media on your content material fabric.

5.1 Understanding the WordPress Editor

The number one tool you use to create and regulate the cloth on your website is the WordPress editor. The editor that became designed and carried out in WordPress five.Zero is also referred to as the block editor or Gutenberg. The basis of the WordPress editor is the idea of blocks, which is probably the vital content material fabric gadgets that you could upload, rearrange, and personalize in your internet web web page. Various types of blocks are available, at the side of text, header, image, list, citation, gallery, video, and extra. The WordPress Handbook has a whole listing of blocks and their functionality.

The WordPress editor is fabricated from numerous sections and components that can help you do various sports activities, like:

The toolbar, that is the horizontal bar on the pinnacle of the editor, has a few buttons and menus that allow you to get admission to 3 fashionable features like publishing or saving your artwork, along with new cloth, and undoing or redoing moves.

Material Section: This is the primary place in which you can use blocks to look and update your fabric. The block toolbar, block sidebar, and block menu assist you to add, delete, and rearrange blocks as well as adjust their settings and homes.

The horizontal bar that looks above every block is known as the "block toolbar," and it has buttons and options that will let you perform excellent operations associated with that block, such formatting, along with a hyperlink, altering the block kind, and aligning it.

Block sidebar: This is the vertical panel that suggests up at the editor's proper facet. It has tabs and sections that allow you to get entry to the block's superior or state-of-the-art settings and options, collectively with style, shade, length, and visibility.

The block menu, which can be accessed thru clicking the 3 dots image at the block toolbar, is a vertical menu that gives numerous alternatives and movements for handling blocks. These embody moving, copying, deleting, and along with reusable blocks.

With the help of the robust and intuitive WordPress editor, you can without problem and adaptably write and exchange your material. You may additionally moreover generate and control any kind of fabric on your website via turning into gifted with the WordPress editor and its blocks.

5.2 Adding and Formatting Text

Since text presents your traffic and clients together with your message, information, or rate, it's far the most famous and essential piece of content material on your internet site. Text may be used for quite more than a few of factors, such expressing your thoughts or ideas, narrating your narrative, introducing your net site, and describing your objects or services. Using the WordPress editor and its blocks, which include and formatting text in your internet website online is a short and clean machine.

You have to do the subsequent movements in case you want to upload and layout textual content for your internet site:

1. Enter your username and password to get entry to your WordPress dashboard with the aid of going to https://yourdomain.Com/wp-admin/ in your browser.

2. Select each Posts > Add New or Pages > Add New from the WordPress dashboard's left sidebar menu, based totally completely at the type of cloth you need to generate.

3. In the "Add become aware of" place, type your turn out to be privy to. Your placed up's or internet internet page's call serves as its call; it should be interest-grabbing, pertinent, and evocative. Along with the browser tab and are attempting to find engine outcomes, your identify appears inside the header of your website.

4. To add a state-of-the-art block to the content material cloth vicinity, click the plus

button or hit the Enter key. A shape of block sorts, which includes paragraph, header, listing, quotation, and so forth, are to be had for choice. Additionally, you may use the hunt bar to look for a block by way of inputting its call or a key-phrase.

five. In the block you have inserted, kind your textual content. In addition to voice dictation and speech popularity software application software like Google Docs Voice Typing or Speechnotes, you may also write or replica your content material material cloth. Additionally, you could perform numerous ordinary duties the usage of keyboard shortcuts. For example, Ctrl+I to italicize, Ctrl+B to ambitious, and Ctrl+K to create a link. By hitting Shift+Alt+H or choosing the Keyboard Shortcuts icon inside the toolbar, you can see the entire listing of keyboard shortcuts.

6. Use the block menu, block sidebar, or block toolbar to format your content material. You may also upload gadgets like links,

photos, or media, as well as adjust the textual content's type, alignment, and style. By deciding on the Edit as HTML opportunity from the block menu or thru using Ctrl+Shift+Alt+M, you may moreover add some HTML tags or CSS code for your text.

Continue consisting of and formatting textual content blocks through following steps four via 6 until all of your records has been delivered. To decorate your content material fabric, you can additionally embody other block sorts like media, format, or widget blocks.

Using the WordPress editor and its blocks, adding and formatting textual content for your net website is a easy and speedy process. By deciding on the Edit or Delete alternative from the block toolbar or block menu, you could moreover change or put off your textual content blocks at any 2nd.

5.Three Incorporating Media into Your Content

Another essential and useful kind of fabric in your internet site is media, which enhances it with interaction, range, and aesthetic enchantment. Media may be used for a choice of things, such demonstrating your thoughts, selling your gadgets or offerings, attractive your goal market, or expressing your creativity. It can take the form of photographs, audio, video, or different types. With the WordPress editor and its blocks, adding media for your article is a short and easy machine.

The tactics indexed beneath need to be determined so that you can consist of media on your content material material:

1. Enter your username and password to access your WordPress dashboard by means of using going to https://yourdomain.Com/wp-admin/ on your browser.

2. Select every Posts > Add New or Pages > Add New from the WordPress dashboard's

left sidebar menu, based at the form of cloth you need to generate.

3. To upload a modern day block to the content fabric vicinity, click on on on the plus button or hit the Enter key. A shape of media block sorts, which include image, audio, video, gallery, and greater, are to be had for desire. By coming into the name or key-phrase of the media block in the seek region, you may additionally look for it.

4. In the block you have inserted, add or choose your media document. By clicking the Upload button, dragging and dropping the report, or copying the URL, you may add your media file from your computer, cell tool, or cloud issuer. By selecting the Media Library button, you may additionally select out your media document from your library, or via choosing the Insert from URL button, you may pick out out it from an outside supply like Unsplash, YouTube, or Spotify.

five. Use the block menu, block sidebar, or block toolbar to make adjustments on your media document. Your media file can be altered in terms of length, orientation, and style. You also can upload extra capabilities like captions, alt text, and hyperlinks. By choosing the Edit button located within the block toolbar, you could moreover use other improving abilties like cropping, rotating, and filtering.

To upload extra media blocks, repeat steps three via five until your fabric is entire. To enhance your media, you could additionally use specific block types as textual content, layout, or widget blocks.

With WordPress' editor and its blocks, which includes media for your article is a simple and speedy manner. By selecting the Edit or Delete alternative from the block toolbar or block menu, you can also trade or get rid of your media blocks at any moment.

You may also use the following media block examples to enhance your content material:

1. You may additionally upload an photograph for your internet web site, which include a picture, a logo, or an icon, the usage of the photograph block. You have three options for selecting a photo: drag and drop an image out of your device or media library, or import an photograph from an outside deliver like Unsplash. Additionally, you could add components like captions, alt textual content, or hyperlinks in your photograph and alter it via using manner of cropping, rotating, or filtering it. The Image Compare block also can be used to reveal the variations among images, which consist of before and after or altered and specific. Examples of picture blocks are supplied inside the WordPress Handbook.

2. You may moreover add an audio record, which includes a track, podcast, or sound impact, to your internet site using the audio block. You have three alternatives for importing audio documents: pick out one out of your media library, add one out of your laptop or tool, or insert one from an outdoor

source like Spotify. Additionally, you may upload abilities like controls, subtitles, or preload alternatives for your audio record in addition to improving it with the useful resource of looping, muting, or reducing it. Moreover, you can create a fixed of audio documents that can be randomly or consecutively played with the aid of the usage of the Playlist block. The WordPress Handbook has numerous times of audio blocks.

three. You may upload a video document on your net website online, which include a film, a lesson, or a testimonial, using the video block. You have 3 options for which encompass video documents: select one from your media library, add one out of your pc or tool, or insert one from an out of doors deliver like YouTube. Additionally, you may upload features like controls, autoplay alternatives, and subtitles on your video clip in addition to modifying it with the resource of cropping, rotating, and filtering it.

Chapter 4: Managing Users And Permissions

In this financial disaster, we're capable of discover ways to manage customers and permissions in WordPress, a famous content cloth cloth management machine (CMS) that powers over forty% of the internet. WordPress allows you to create and manage top notch sorts of customers, every with excellent roles and skills. You can also set permissions and privacy settings for your net web site, consisting of who can access, edit, or touch upon your content material cloth. By information a manner to control clients and permissions, you can ensure the protection and functionality of your WordPress net website on-line.

6.1 User Roles and Capabilities

The six primary individual roles defined with the aid of using WordPress are Contributor, Author, Super Admin, Administrator, Editor, and Subscriber. The sports that every person role is capable of doing on the internet web site are decided by way of way in their set of talents. For instance, an Administrator has the functionality to perform any administrative characteristic, such as problem modifications, plugin installations, and man or woman deletions, even as a Subscriber is restricted to managing their non-public profile and region viewing. Each man or woman characteristic's primary capabilities are enumerated in the table beneath:

User Role Capabilities

Super Admin Has get right of entry to to the complete community of internet sites in a WordPress multisite installation. Can create, edit, delete, and control net web sites, clients, topics, plugins, and settings.

Administrator Has get right of entry to to all of the administrative capabilities of a unmarried WordPress website. Can create, edit, delete, and control posts, pages, media, comments, instructions, tags, clients, topics, plugins, and settings.

Editor Can create, edit, delete, and manage posts, pages, media, and feedback of any man or woman. Can additionally manage instructions and tags. Cannot get proper of entry to themes, plugins, or settings.

Author Can create, edit, delete, and manipulate their non-public posts and media. Can furthermore view feedback, but cannot moderate them. Cannot get proper of entry to pages, lessons, tags, issues, plugins, or settings.

Contributor Can create and edit their very very own posts, but can not put up them. Can moreover view feedback, but can not moderate them. Cannot access media, pages, lessons, tags, problems, plugins, or settings.

Subscriber Can only manage their very personal profile and reflect onconsideration on the website on line. Cannot get admission to each different function

You can assign a person characteristic to each person at the identical time as you create or edit them in the Users section of your WordPress dashboard. You can also exchange the patron function of any user at any time, besides for the Super Admin function, that would handiest be granted by way of the usage of every other Super Admin. You also can create custom individual roles and competencies the use of plugins, collectively with User Role Editor or Members.

6.2 Adding and Managing Users

You must choose out Users > create New out of your dashboard so that you can create a brand new consumer for your WordPress net website. You'll be furnished with a form to fill up with the individual's records, which includes position, email, password, and username. Additionally, you have got were given the option of sending the purchaser's login statistics in an electronic mail be conscious. Click Add New User to create the user after completing the shape.

You have to go to Users > All Users to your dashboard which will manipulate modern-day customers. All of the clients on your internet web site can be verified, together with their username, name, electronic mail cope with, feature, and quantity of posts. To find out a positive client, the usage of the filters or the hunt difficulty. Additionally, you could carry out bulk operations on numerous customers, such emailing, role-changing, and deletion. Hover your cursor over someone's username and pick out out Edit to make changes. A display with the individual's information, collectively with name, e mail, password, function, and profile, will seem. By deciding on Delete at the bottom of the display display screen, you can moreover dispose of a purchaser.

6.Three Setting Permissions and Privacy

WordPress offers you the functionality to manage your website on-line's privacy and permissions, together with who can see, update, and comment on your fabric. These alternatives are positioned within the

Dashboard's options section. Among the primary configurations are:

General: This segment lets in you to modify the language, time place, electronic mail cope with, URL, slogan, and contact of your internet site. Additionally, you may determine what function someone may additionally moreover have through manner of default when they test in on your website on-line and whether or not or not to permit each person to achieve this.

Reading: This is in which you configure the RSS feed, are seeking for engine visibility, range of articles consistent with internet web page, and homepage. Additionally, you've got were given manipulate over whether or no longer or not search engines like google and yahoo crawl your internet website, which also can have an impact on its website on line site visitors and rating.

Discussion: This is in that you configure the parameters for feedback, together with who may also moreover depart comments, how they'll be vetted, how they seem, and what indicators are issued. Pingbacks and trackbacks are symptoms that your net internet web site gets even as a few different internet site connects to cloth that you have created. You can also pick out to set off or disable them.

Media: You might also additionally furthermore configure the default dimensions for pics, films, and audio files you upload for your internet website right proper here. Additionally, you've got got the selection of grouping your media documents into folders in step with the month or the 12 months.

Permalinks: This is in which you configure the submit, net page, beauty, and tag URL systems. Numerous preset choices are to be had for desire, which includes numeric, located up name, day and talk to, month and call, and smooth. Using tags like %postname%, %elegance%, or %writer%, you can also layout your private particular shape. Your website's search engine optimization and usefulness may be advanced by means of way of selecting a permalink structure this is each descriptive and easy to apply.

Chapter 5: Search Engine Optimization

In this bankruptcy, we are able to learn how to optimize your WordPress internet web web page for search engines like google and yahoo, collectively with Google, Bing, or Yahoo. Search engine optimization (are seeking engine advertising) is the manner of improving the brilliant and quantity of site visitors to your internet web page from natural search outcomes. Organic are looking for for consequences are folks who appear without a doubt on the seek engine stop result pages (SERPs), with out shopping for advertisements. By optimizing your net website for search engine optimization, you can increase your web site's visibility, relevance, and authority in your goal keywords and goal market. You also can improve your internet site online's client enjoy, ordinary performance, and safety.

7.1 The Importance of seek engine advertising for Your Website seek engine advertising and advertising is important in your net site due to the truth that it may help you in acquiring some of advantages, on the side of:

More web page traffic: are looking for engine advertising also can help you in reaching a better search engine score for your preferred key phrases, with the intention to draw more customers on your website. A Backlinko studies states that the top cease end result on Google receives 31.7% of hits, at the same time due to the fact the tenth surrender result gets simply three.1%. As such, getting a higher role might also have a huge impact on the quantity and great of your site visitors.

More conversions: You may additionally moreover growth the form of site visitors that turn out to be clients, subscribers, or fans with the aid of using are searching for engine marketing. You might also additionally offer applicable, useful, and captivating content material that aligns with the quest motive and target marketplace expectancies through the use of optimizing your internet web page for search engines like google. To urge clients to carry out the important action to your net internet page, you could also lease calls to movement (CTAs) which is probably appealing and easy to apprehend.

More credibility: seek engine advertising and advertising and marketing may also assist you in setting up authority and recall in your brand and internet site. You might also moreover speak to your target market that your net web site is dependable, beneficial, and sincere with the beneficial resource of placing higher in the SERPs. Additionally, you may utilize search engine advertising and marketing techniques like link constructing, social media marketing, and on-line reviews to beautify the popularity and recognition of your net web page internal your vicinity and place.

More insights: search engine marketing can also offer you with insightful facts on the behavior of your target marketplace, the effectiveness of your website, and the techniques used by your combatants. Various metrics and facts, together with website online site traffic sources, key phrases, soar fee, conversion charge, and rating positions, can be tracked and analyzed the use of search engine optimization equipment like Google Analytics, Google Search Console, or Bing Webmaster Tools. Additionally, you could do competition analysis, net internet web page audits, and key-phrase studies the use of search engine advertising gear like Ahrefs, Moz, and SEMrush.

These are maximum of the number one justifications for why search engine optimization topics for your net site. Your net internet web page's exposure, relevance, authority, customer experience, widespread ordinary overall performance, and protection can also all be more suited via optimizing it for search engines.

7.2 Optimizing Content for Search Engines

Optimizing your content fabric for search engines like google like google and yahoo is one of the maximum essential factors of search engine optimization. The textual content, photographs, movies, audio, and infographics that you positioned up in your website are all considered varieties of content material fabric. Your internet internet web page's content cloth is what draws in website on line visitors and maintains them involved. It also lets in search engines like google and yahoo apprehend and prioritize your net internet site. Thus, producing specific, applicable, and extremely good content cloth is essential for search engine advertising and marketing normal overall performance.

You need to adhere to nice fantastic practices that allows you to optimize your content material fabric fabric for serps, along with:

Keyword research: This is the act of identifying and comparing the phrases and expressions that people for your target audience use at the same time as seeking out your scenario, area of know-how, or area. By doing key-word research, you may higher apprehend the quest cause, name for, and issue of your goal key phrases and offer content material cloth that meets the expectancies and needs of your target market. To find out useful and relevant phrases in your content material cloth, you can do keyword studies the use of seo gadget like Ubersuggest, Google Keyword Planner, and AnswerThePublic.

Content manufacturing: The manner of creating and disseminating information, solutions, and cost to your target marketplace is called content material introduction. Creating content fabric fabric also can help you be a part of and collect a dating together with your target market whilst showcasing your character, creativity, and vicinity of expertise. To generate content fabric that fits your state of affairs, region, and target market, you may rent an entire lot of formats and content material fabric sorts, consisting of weblog posts, articles, courses, tutorials, critiques, case studies, testimonials, ebooks, podcasts, movies, webinars, and infographics.

Material Optimization: This is the approach of refining and boosting your fabric in order that engines like google like google and yahoo like google and your goal market will discover it extra relevant, beneficial, and interesting. Your cloth's clarity, clarity, and shape may also additionally additionally all be greater suitable with content fabric optimization, which also can assist you strategically and organically encompass your goal key phrases and related phrases. To optimize your content material cloth fabric for serps, you may use search engine optimization techniques collectively with identify tags, meta descriptions, headings, subheadings, paragraphs, lists, photographs, alt text, links, anchor textual content, and schema markup.

Here are some key moves and encouraged techniques for search engine optimization of your content material. You can offer your target market and search engines rate and delight through generating unique, high-quality content material cloth.

7.Three Using seek engine marketing Plugins Effectively

Effective use of are looking for engine advertising and marketing plugins is a critical trouble of search engine optimization. Installing and activating software software application extensions in your WordPress internet website to beautify and streamline your seek engine advertising efforts is referred to as an are looking for engine advertising and marketing plugin. You might also furthermore carry out some of seo operations and responsibilities with the aid of are seeking for engine advertising plugins, together with analytics, link constructing, social media advertising, internet web page audits, content optimization, and key-phrase research.

The following are a a number of the most nicely-desired and powerful WordPress search engine optimization plugins:

Yoast search engine optimization: One of the maximum popular and dependable WordPress are seeking engine marketing plugins is Yoast search engine optimization. With its many functions and system, alongside aspect seo evaluation, clarity evaluation, XML sitemaps, breadcrumbs, canonical URLs, meta tags, schema markup, social community integration, and extra, Yoast seo will let you in optimizing your website for search engines like google.

Rank Math: Rank Math is an extra nicely-appreciated and function-rich WordPress seo plugin. With its array of features and equipment, which include key-word pointers, content material evaluation, rich snippets, XML sitemaps, redirections, 404 reveal, internal and outdoor links, social community integration, and similarly, Rank Math may also additionally help you in enhancing the search engine optimization of your internet site.

All in One seek engine advertising and advertising: Another famous and characteristic-rich WordPress search engine optimization plugin is All in One seo. With skills and device which incorporates XML sitemaps, robots.Txt,.Htaccess, meta tags, schema markup, social media integration, and more, All in One are seeking for engine advertising permit you to enhance the search engine marketing of your net site.

To optimize your WordPress net internet site on line for search engines like google, you can employ a number of the most well-known seo plugins. You can streamline and automate your seo manner and decorate your effects via way of making right use of search engine optimization plugins.

Chapter 6: Enhancing User Experience With Widgets And Menus

In this financial ruin, we are capable of discover ways to beautify the character enjoy of your WordPress internet web site with widgets and menus. Widgets and menus are abilties that permit you to customise and set up your internet page's layout, content fabric, and functionality. By using widgets and menus, you could decorate the arrival, usability, and accessibility of your internet website online on line to your traffic.

8.1 Customizing Your Site with Widgets

You may additionally furthermore add widgets—small content material or capability blocks—to the header, footer, sidebar, or every other widget-prepared phase of your internet site. A e-newsletter signup shape, modern articles, training, tags, are attempting to find container, calendar, social network icons, and more may additionally all be confirmed using widgets. With the usage of widgets, you may enhance the rate, content material fabric, and interactivity which you provide to your clients whilst also adding dynamic and captivating factors in your internet internet site online.

Go to Appearance > Widgets for your dashboard to characteristic widgets to your internet website. A listing of widget areas is demonstrated at the proper, at the same time as a listing of available widgets is displayed at the left. Any widget may be moved from the left to any widget place at the proper with the useful resource of dragging and dropping it, and you can additionally trade its alternatives, become aware of, and content fabric. By clicking at the name bar of any widget, you may additionally alternate, put off, or reorganize it. Additionally, you could preview and edit your widgets in actual time the usage of the Customizer.

WordPress comes with a number of primary widgets that you can use to your net internet website, however you can moreover set up and activate plugins like Jetpack, SiteOrigin

Widgets Bundle, or Elementor that provide more widgets. Additionally, you could use code, which include PHP, HTML, CSS, or JavaScript, or plugins, like Widget Options or Widget Shortcode, to construct your private particular widgets.

eight.2 Creating and Managing Menus

Links to the pages, articles, schooling, tags, and different custom URLs on your net site may be tested thru menus, which are navigational additives. Menus might also help you in structuring and organizing the material on your net net web page and facilitate finding and getting access to content fabric for customers. By providing concise and illustrative connections on your internet web site's pages, menus also can help beautify your internet net page's are searching for engine advertising.

You need to go to Appearance > Menus in your dashboard with a view to assemble and control menus. You might be offered with a panel that permits you to characteristic, regulate, and put off menus similarly to installation them in menu positions and display them the usage of widgets. You need to provide your menu a call and then pick out out construct Menu so that it will build it. Then, the use of the left panels, you could upload gadgets like pages, articles, classes, tags, and custom hyperlinks for your menu. To drift, indent, or delete an object out of your menu, just drag & drop it. Expanding an object allows you to alternate its CSS training, label, and phone assets. Depending on the settings for your scenario remember range, you may pick out out a menu function from the bottom left panel after adding and organizing your menu objects. These opportunities consist of vital, secondary, and footer menus. Additionally, you may preview and edit your menus in actual time using the Customizer.

You might also use WordPress to assemble severa menus for fantastic makes use of and locations, however you can additionally utilize plugins like Mega Menu, Responsive Menu, or

Max Mega Menu to boom the functionality and customization of your menus. Additionally, you could use code, such HTML, CSS, or JavaScript, or plugins, like Menu Image or Menu Icons, to layout your private precise menus.

8.Three Improving Navigation for Visitors

In addition to the use of widgets and menus to assist traffic navigate your internet website more resultseasily, you may additionally use more techniques and great practices to enhance the person revel in to your internet website, like:

Breadcrumb Navigation: This is a supplementary navigation detail to your internet site that shows the modern-day net internet page or located up's hierarchical course. Using breadcrumb navigation can also additionally make it less difficult for customers to navigate your internet web web site and discover their current region in addition to the decide or previous web page. By imparting relevant and semantic connections for your net web site on-line's pages, breadcrumb navigation may additionally moreover help your website's search engine optimization. To add breadcrumb navigation on your internet web website, utilize plugins like Rank Math, Yoast search engine optimization, or Breadcrumb NavXT.

The navigation function called pagination separates the content material fabric fabric of your internet internet site on line into many pages and gives links to permit customers pass amongst them. If you have got a whole lot of articles or objects for your net website, pagination may additionally make it less complex and similarly green for customers to get admission to and eat the material for your internet web page. By speeding up loading instances and making your net web site an awful lot much less complex to crawl, pagination might also additionally moreover help increase the hunt engine advertising of your internet site. To add pagination to your internet web page, employ plugins like WP-PageNavi, WP-Paginate, or WP-PostRatings.

Search Box: This navigational feature shall we clients type a time period or phrase to find out pertinent statistics or fabric for your net internet site online. Using a are attempting to find field also can assist customers discover what they may be looking for fast and precisely at the same time as also saving time and effort. By providing facts approximately the search conduct and options of your users, a seek field can also help beautify the seo of your internet web page. Plugins like Relevanssi, Ajax Search Lite, and SearchWP can be used to increase and decorate the search abilties in your internet website online.

Chapter 7: Understanding And Utilizing Blogging Features

In this chapter, we're able to discover ways to use WordPress as a running a blog platform, and the way to create and manage enticing and effective blog posts. Blogging is a form of online content material cloth introduction and conversation that allows you to percentage your thoughts, opinions, critiques, or know-how together along with your target audience. Blogging will let you particular yourself, show off your information, build your brand, expand your audience, and monetize your web web web page.

nine.1 Starting a Blog on WordPress

With over forty% of the net taking walks on it, WordPress is one of the most widely used and high-quality taking walks a weblog systems global. WordPress gives a number of gear and options that make starting and maintaining a blog clean and adaptable, which includes:

The layout and layout templates that dictate the appearance and enjoy of your net internet page are referred to as project subjects. Thousands of loose and paid topics are to be had on WordPress on the manner to select from, primarily based in your preferences, style, and vicinity of information. Additionally, you could use code, such CSS or PHP, or the Customizer to modify and alter your subject matter.

Plugins: Software extensions that offer your internet net website online greater abilities and abilities are referred to as plugins. Depending for your necessities and desires, WordPress gives you with over 50,000 free and paid plugins that you can set up and set off in your net site. Additionally, you could use code, on the aspect of PHP, HTML, CSS, or JavaScript, to accumulate your very own particular plugins.

The content fabric fabric portions you can use to construct and modify your weblog pages and posts are known as blocks. WordPress comes with a block editor known as Gutenberg that lets you create, rearrange, and customize a huge fashion of block types, collectively with headers, paragraphs, lists, tables, pix, movies, and buttons. To upload additional blocks on your net internet website online, you can moreover make use of plugins like Elementor, Jetpack, and SiteOrigin Widgets Bundle.

Configuring and handling many regions of your internet site, which includes favored, writing, reading, verbal exchange, media, and permalinks, is possible through the settings menu. Your dashboard's Settings location is wherein you may see and modify your settings.

nine.2 Crafting Engaging Blog Posts

Writing exciting and useful weblog entries is maximum of the maximum vital elements of walking a blog. The man or woman articles or entries you submit for your net web page for readers to observe, remark on, or percent are called blog posts. Blog entries may also help you in connecting together with your goal marketplace and constructing a dating with them through presenting them solutions, charge, and facts.

You must adhere to some incredible practices in case you want to put in writing blog entries which can be exciting and beneficial, like:

Selecting A Subject: The first diploma in writing a weblog put up is choosing a subject. You need to pick a subject that aligns along facet your strong aspect, fashion, and purpose this is applicable, appealing, and useful to your audience. To discover and provide you with mission ideas, you could employ a number of device and resources, consisting of thoughts mapping, keyword studies, competition evaluation, target market comments, and brainstorming.

Developing A Headline: The 2d stage in writing a blog submit is growing a headline. You should create a call in your weblog article that captures the essence of the content material fabric and its essential elements in a easy, succinct, and attractive way. To enlarge and decorate your headline, you may use masses of formulae and strategies, such the use of questions, figures, electricity phrases, or emotional triggers. To create and inspect your discover, you may additionally make use of system like Portent Title Maker, Sharethrough find out Analyzer, and CoSchedule Headline Analyzer.

Writing An Introduction: The 0.33 degree in producing a blog put up is writing an advent. It's imperative which you craft an engrossing, academic, and convincing starting that piques the interest of your readers and encourages them to hold studying your weblog article. To compose and beautify your advent, you may employ a number of techniques and components, which encompass a promise, a question, a statistic, a tale, or a citation.

The fourth diploma in writing a weblog put up is to put in writing the body. The body of your blog put up ought to consist of substantial, realistic, and fascinating cloth that conveys the item's center idea. To compose and decorate your body, you could use quite some content material paperwork and types, inclusive of text, pix, motion photographs, audio, and infographics. To compose and installation your body, you can moreover appoint quite some codecs and techniques, such lists, bullet factors, paragraphs, headers, and subheadings.

Composing A Concluding Statement: The 5th degree in writing a weblog positioned up is writing a stop. The prevent of your blog article ought to be memorable, huge, and practical. It want to furthermore recap the important aspect mind and commands protected and nudge readers to take the subsequent motion. To growth and decorate your completing, you could use lots of strategies and elements, this sort of summary, a query, a suggestion, a CTA, or a PS.

9.Three Utilizing Categories and Tags Effectively

The inexperienced use of lessons and tags is a important thing of strolling a weblog. You can also additionally categorize and set up your weblog entries normal with their venture, subject, or key-word the use of the kinds and tags device. Your target market and search engines like google will discover and access your blog articles greater with out issues if you use categories and tags to help you arrange and manipulate the statistics to your website.

You have to adhere to best incredible practices in case you need to use instructions and tags properly, along with:

Using Categories: Categories are the full-size, overarching subjects that outline the number one goal and scope of your website and weblog. To put together your weblog content material material fabric into amazing elements or troubles, like information, reviews, tutorials, or recommendation, utilize training. The Posts > Categories vicinity of your dashboard is wherein you could installation and maintain your lessons. Every weblog submit also can have a category assigned to it the use of the block editor's Document > Categories panel. There want to fine be five to ten instructions each net web page, and you need to utilize them carefully and selectively.

Using Tags: Tags are the perfect, granular key terms that constitute the distinct elements and contents of your blog entries. Tags can be used to attract interest to and intensify certain subtopics, skills, or additives of your blog entries, together with WordPress, search engine optimization, plugins, and widgets. From your dashboard, go to the Posts > Tags location to create and modify your tags. Additionally, you can tag each blog placed up the usage of the block editor's Document > Tags panel. You may be revolutionary and free in conjunction with your tag use, the usage of as many as are pertinent and appropriate for each weblog article.

Employing Hierarchy: Your instructions and tags are prepared in a hierarchy. Your net website on line and blog can also have a logical, regular navigation system in case you appoint hierarchy to construct it. Subcategories and nested layers for your instructions, like WordPress > Plugins > search engine optimization, can be created using determine and little one training. Additionally, you can appoint tags to interlink and flow into-reference your blog entries in other lessons, such plugins, WordPress, and seo.

Chapter 8: Troubleshooting And Maintenance

In this bankruptcy, we're capable of learn how to troubleshoot and preserve your WordPress website, and the way to repair common problems and problems that could stand up. Troubleshooting and maintenance are essential capabilitics and practices in order to allow you to ensure the protection, simple usual overall performance, and functionality of your net web page, and save you or remedy any mistakes, bugs, or conflicts that might affect your internet site online.

10.1 Common Issues and How to Fix Them

Although WordPress is a robust and reliable platform, faults and issues might also additionally though upward thrust up for plenty of motives, together with mismatched plugins, issues, or upgrades; damaged files or databases; server or web hosting problems; or purchaser errors. The following are a number of the most widespread troubles and answers:

White Screen Of Death: When you attempt to visit your dashboard or net website online, a smooth white display screen suggests and stops you from seeing or doing some thing. A large range of things, together with a entire RAM restrict, a malfunctioning plugin or difficulty, a syntax mistake, or malware infestation, can also bring about the "white show of lack of existence." The following fixes may also assist you treatment white show of loss of existence:

1. You may additionally enhance your reminiscence restrict by using which include the line define('WP_MEMORY_LIMIT', '256M'); on your wp-config.Personal home internet web page record.

2. Using cPanel or FTP, rename your plugins folder to some thing wonderful, such plugins_old, to deactivate your plugins.

3. Using cPanel or FTP, rename your cutting-edge subject matter folder to some aspect wonderful, such theme_old, to exchange to the default problem matter.

four. Look for any grammatical mistakes to your code, together with missing prices, brackets, or semicolons, and use a code editor or validator to accurate them.

5. Check your net internet site on line for malware and viruses, then do away with them the usage of a safety plugin or provider like MalCare, Wordfence, or Sucuri.

6. Error organising a database connection: This errors message stops you from loading your website or dashboard at the same time as your internet site on-line is not capable of create a connection to your database. A quantity of things, along with wrong database credentials, broken databases, and server or internet website hosting issues, would possibly bring about an mistakes whilst searching for to create a database connection. One feasible approach to the trouble putting in area a database connection is to attempt the subsequent fixes:

7. By improving your wp-config.Personal home internet page document and making that the settings for DB_NAME, DB_USER, DB_PASSWORD, and DB_HOST are accurate and correspond to the ones furnished by way of your net web hosting provider, you can verify and trade your database credentials.

8. To repair your database, visit http://yourdomain.Com/wp-admin/maint/restore.Php after together with the street define('WP_ALLOW_REPAIR', actual); in your wp-config.Personal domestic net page report.

9. Make contact together with your web hosting enterprise and request that they have got a look at and remedy any server or hosting issues (along side overload, downtime, or configuration) that could be affecting your database connection.

Error 404 no longer positioned: When you attempt to visit an internet page or put up that is both nonexistent, has been relocated, or has been deleted, you could get a 404 no longer located errors message alongside aspect a default or custom errors internet web page. A 404 no longer determined mistakes can be the prevent cease result of many things, including broken hyperlinks, lacking or relocated files, and defective permalinks. You may additionally try the subsequent fixes to resolve the 404 no longer determined errors:

1. Reset your permalinks thru using choosing Save Changes without changing some thing underneath Settings > Permalinks for your dashboard.

2. Restore your deleted or lacking files the usage of cPanel or FTP, or by means of the use of a backup plugin or organization like VaultPress, BackupBuddy, or UpdraftPlus.

3. Use a plugin or tool, like Screaming Frog, Link Checker, or Broken Link Checker, to restore your damaged hyperlinks with the useful resource of finding and changing folks that aspect to pages or posts that don't exist.

These are maximum of the most everyday issues at the thing of solutions. Debugging, errors logs, forums, and useful useful resource are only some different gadget and strategies you may use to pick out and clear up any more problems that might be plaguing your internet web page.

10.2 Regular Maintenance Practices

While diagnosing and resolving troubles is vital, it is advanced to avoid problems altogether. For this cause, regular WordPress net website protection is vital as it can help you hold your internet site on line stable, short, and operational while moreover warding off any possible troubles or disputes. Among the regular maintenance techniques you want to carry out for your internet site are:

1. Updating the middle, plugins, and problem topics of WordPress: One of the maximum vital and essential safety techniques is updating the WordPress center, plugins, and topics. This also can help you

assure the protection, functionality, and compatibility of your website and address any insects or protection flaws which can exist within the software software. By choosing Update Now or Update All below Dashboard > Updates in your dashboard, you could update the center WordPress software software application in addition to plugins and subjects. Moreover, you may use a plugin or piece of code to allow computerized updates for your WordPress middle, plugins, and issues.

2. Creating a WordPress internet website backup: Creating a backup of your WordPress net site is each other essential and primary protection gadget that will help you protect the information and files to your internet site and get higher them in the occasion that they may be misplaced, corrupted, or broken for any cause—which includes hacking, mistakes, or injuries. Using a plugin or provider like UpdraftPlus, BackupBuddy, or VaultPress, or manually exporting your database and files using phpMyAdmin and FTP or cPanel, you

can backup your WordPress internet web website online.

three. Optimizing your WordPress database: You may additionally additionally decrease the scale and clutter of your database and beautify the speed, effectiveness, and performance of your website via the usage of optimizing your WordPress database. This is some one of a kind crucial and fantastic preservation technique. Using a plugin or device like WP-Optimize, WP-Sweep, or phpMyAdmin, you can optimize your WordPress database thru clearing out any extraneous or redundant facts like revisions, drafts, junk mail, garbage, transients, or tables.

four. Verifying and defensive your WordPress net web page: Another vital and beneficial renovation system for WordPress websites is scanning and safeguarding them. This will assist you guard against malware, viruses, and distinct threats that would undermine or harm your internet internet site, further to defend its statistics and documents from unauthorised get right of access to or alteration. Using a plugin or provider like Wordfence, MalCare, or Sucuri, you can show and take a look at your WordPress internet internet web page for threats and viruses, then delete or block them.

These are the diverse ordinary renovation strategies you need to have a study to your net website on-line. To hold and beautify your net website on-line, you could additionally hire different techniques and recommendations like cleansing your cache, verifying your links, trying your paperwork, or searching over your analytics.

10.Three Backing Up Your WordPress Site

One of the most critical and suggested safety techniques for WordPress websites is developing backups. These can also additionally help you protect your net web page's facts and documents and restore them inside the event that they will be misplaced, corrupted, or broken for any purpose—together with hacking, errors, or accidents. Making a backup of your WordPress internet site can also permit you check or take a look at with it without impacting the live version, further to drift or clone it to a unique area or server.

You ought to backup each your documents and your database if you want to restore your WordPress net web site. All of the statistics and configurations in your net web page, collectively with posts, pages, feedback, clients, options, and greater, are stored on your database. All of the code and fabric in your internet site, collectively with problem subjects, plugins, tune, video, and image documents, are blanketed to your documents.

Using a plugin or provider, or manually exporting your database and files, are the two number one techniques available for backing up your WordPress net website online. Every approach has benefits and disadvantages, so that you may additionally select out the simplest that excellent fits your requirements and tastes.

10.Three.1 Utilizing a provider or plugin

The best and maximum practical approach to backup your WordPress internet site is to apply a plugin or provider. These may additionally automate and streamline the backup technique and provide loads of features and alternatives, such as scheduling, storage, encryption, compression, recovery, and further. You might also moreover moreover make use of some of nicely-liked and honest services and plugins to backup your WordPress internet site, along with:

With greater than three million active installs, UpdraftPlus is one of the most famous and reliable backup plugins for WordPress. UpdraftPlus offers a range of gear and options, together with scheduling, garage, encryption, compression, restoration, and further, that will help you in backing up and restoring your WordPress internet website online. UpdraftPlus lets in you to backup your internet internet web page on your nearby computer or to some of outside internet web web sites, which incorporates Dropbox, Google Drive, Amazon S3, and FTP. Additionally, you could use UpdraftPlus to move or clone your internet web page to a superb area or server, further to restore it from any backup.

BackupBuddy: With more than 500,000 active installs, BackupBuddy is however some different properly-liked and feature-rich backup plugin for WordPress. BackupBuddy presents lots of gadget and alternatives, which includes scheduling, garage, encryption, compression, restoration, and extra, to assist you in backing up, restoring, and migrating your WordPress internet web web page. BackupBuddy lets in you to backup your net website online to a community drive or to some of a ways flung websites, together with Dropbox, Google Drive, Amazon S3, FTP, BackupBuddy Stash, and so forth. BackupBuddy also can be used emigrate or clone your internet web page to a one of a kind place or server, in addition to to restore your website from any backup.

VaultPress: Powered through way of Jetpack, VaultPress is a complicated WordPress backup solution. With capabilities and options which includes actual-time backup, storage, encryption, compression, recuperation, and extra, VaultPress can help you in backing up, restoring, and safeguarding your WordPress internet website online. With VaultPress, you could lower lower lower back up your internet web site to every your close by computer and the VaultPress cloud. Additionally, you could bypass or clone your website to a one in all a type location or server, similarly to restore it from any backup the use of VaultPress.

These are among the most nicely-preferred and honest services and plugins for backing up WordPress web internet sites. To backup your internet site, you can moreover hire extra plugins and offerings like Duplicator, WPBackItUp, or BackWPup.

10.Three.2 Manually exporting your database and documents

The more complicated and trade method of backing up your WordPress internet internet site is to manually export your database and documents, which takes greater time, strive, and technical knowledge. It may, however, additionally provide you greater freedom and manipulate over your backup approach and can help you backup your net internet site on-line without the want for any offerings or plugins.

FTP or cPanel and phpMyAdmin are the 2 equipment you will want to manually export your files and database. A internet-based software program known as phpMyAdmin lets you access and manipulate your database. You can get proper of entry to and manipulate your documents with the use of packages like cPanel or FTP. These packages will let you export your files and database to an out of doors disk or cloud service, in addition for your nearby computer.

Use phpMyAdmin to manually export your database through following those steps:

1. Go into your web web hosting account and use the manipulate panel to get proper of get right of entry to to phpMyAdmin.

2. Choose your WordPress database inside the sidebar on the left.

3. Select Export from the principle menu.

4. Select all the tables via selecting the Custom opportunity.

five. Select the compression method and the SQL format.

6. To save the record in your personal computer, click on Go.

In order to export your files manually over FTP or cPanel, you need to do the following movements:

1. Go into your web hosting account and use your manage panel to get proper of access to FTP or cPanel.

2. Go to your WordPress internet internet page's root listing, it's frequently referred to as public_html or www.

3. Choose each report and folder, containing.Htaccess, wp-content material material, and wp-config.Php.

four. You also can add them to a specific region or download them for your close by pc.

five. To manually export your files and database, test these instructions. You may additionally export your files and database using various equipment or strategies like SSH or WP-CLI.

Chapter 9: Updates And Compatibility

Maintaining an up to date internet website on line is not pretty much introducing new talents or aesthetic changes; it is a vital exercise for ensuring robust security and gold contemporary functionality. In the dynamic environment of Word Press, this assignment is even greater massive. Regular updates of the middle software application, venture topics, and plugins are crucial, but the approach needs to be methodical and nicely-informed. It's now not a mere depend of hitting the 'update' button and hoping for the extremely good. A strategic plan, thorough records of compatibility problems, and a scientific approach are critical for a smooth and a success replace.

Before Updating: The Preparation Phase

Comprehensive Backup: Initiating updates without a safety net is a risky enterprise. Always begin through the usage of growing a entire backup of your net web site. This should encompass your database, all Word

Press documents, issue subjects, and plugins. A whole backup ensures that, inside the occasion of an update causing issues, you've got a dependable fallback to repair your internet web page to its previous state. Consider the usage of automated backup solutions that often hold your net site's facts, lowering the chance of data loss.

Compatibility Checks: One of the most commonplace motives of positioned up-replace issues is compatibility conflicts. Before applying any updates, very well take a look at the compatibility of latest versions collectively along with your present day Word Press setup. This includes verifying whether or not or no longer the updates paintings properly together with your contemporary model of Word Press and checking for capacity conflicts with different set up plugins or subjects. Most builders offer special compatibility records, that is beneficial for this approach. Ignoring this step can result in damaged functionality or maybe entire net website online crashes.

Utilizing a Staging Environment: The first-rate way to assume and save you post-update issues is with the resource of using a staging environment this is largely a replica of your live internet page, serving as a sorting out floor in which you could successfully enforce updates with none danger for your stay net web page This surroundings is good for recognizing and addressing problems in advance than they have an effect to your prevent-customers. A staging environment can be set up manually or via numerous net web hosting services that provide this feature.

Updating Process: The Execution Stage

Updating the WordPress Core: Begin the replace machine with the WordPress center. The middle updates are released to introduce new capabilities, restore bugs, and cope with protection vulnerabilities. Keep an eye fixed constant in your WordPress dashboard for notifications regarding new releases. Before updating, make certain that your web page's backups are latest and whole.

Sequential Theme and Plugin Updates: After the middle update, recognition to your subject matters and plugins. These factors of your net net web page are simply as crucial and can have large implications for your internet site online's capability and safety. Update themes and plugins sequentially – separately – to without troubles isolate any problems which can upward thrust up. This workout allows for a managed environment in which the impact of every replace can be monitored and managed.

Functionality Checks: Once all updates are finished, an extensive assessment of the website is important. Navigate thru specific pages, interact with severa functionalities which includes forms, buttons, and hyperlinks, and ensure that each one factors are operating as supposed. This post-update test permits in identifying any not noted issues and assures that the individual revel in stays unaffected.

After Updating: The Monitoring Phase

Issue Resolution: Despite careful training, issues can nevertheless rise up. If you stumble upon any issues placed up-update, your first step need to be to seek advice from the backup made preceding to the updates. Restoring the internet site to its preceding model can be a quick method to revert any vital troubles. Incompatibility among unique plugins or topics is a common problem; achieving out to the respective useful resource businesses can offer you with the crucial steerage for decision.

Ongoing Monitoring: In the times following the updates, maintain a vigilant eye in your net site's ordinary performance and functionality. Some problems won't be proper away obvious and can floor through the years. Regular tracking allows for early detection and quick movement to rectify any rising issues.

Documenting Updates: Maintaining a log of all updates is a exercise regularly left out however quite useful. Record information of every replace, at the aspect of the date, version quantity, and any incredible adjustments or issues encountered. This documentation becomes a valuable beneficial aid for future updates, troubleshooting, and audits. It moreover permits in monitoring the information of modifications, which may be critical for diagnosing prolonged-time period ordinary overall performance tendencies or recurring troubles.

By adopting this complete method to updating your WordPress web page, you now not only make sure its protection and functionality but also make a contribution to its ordinary trendy performance and purchaser revel in. Regular updates, dealt with with due diligence, are fundamental to the long-term fitness and success of your net website online.

Security Practices

In the digital realm, the protection of your WordPress internet web site is paramount. This isn't quite masses safeguarding your very personal information however additionally about shielding the sensitive information of your website traffic. With the developing sophistication of cyber threats, strong safety practices are more critical than ever. This multiplied section will delve into the depths of essential protection skills which incorporates developing and coping with robust passwords, enforcing -element authentication, deciding on reliable concern matters and plugins, and efficaciously the use of protection plugins.

Strong Passwords: The Foundation of Security

Crafting Unbreakable Passwords: The cornerstone of website safety is a sturdy password. It's your first line of protection inside the direction of unauthorized get proper of get entry to to. A strong password need to be a complicated concoction of as a minimum 12 characters, blending better and reduce case letters, numbers, and logos. The secret is to keep away from predictable styles and resultseasily guessable information like names, birthdays, or common phrases. Think of your password as a very precise thriller code that guards the doorway for your virtual nation.

The Role of Password Managers: Managing a plethora of complex passwords can be daunting. This is wherein password managers come into play. These gear aren't certainly vaults for storing passwords; they're sophisticated systems that would generate and retrieve complicated passwords at a moment's word. By the usage of a password supervisor, you alleviate the weight of remembering each password whilst retaining a excessive stage of safety at some point of all debts.

Regular Password Refreshes: In the dynamic panorama of the net, ordinary updates for your passwords are a essential protection exercising. Especially in the wake of a suspected protection breach, changing your passwords may be a clean but powerful device to resecure your internet web page on line. Think of it as a periodic renewal of your digital locks.

Two-Factor Authentication (2FA): A Double Shield

Implementing 2FA: Two-element authentication (2FA) affords a huge layer of protection, performing as a double-take a look at to make certain that the character seeking to get admission to your account is actually you. This approach includes some thing you apprehend (your password) and a few factor you have got were given (a textual content message, electronic mail, authenticator app, or bodily token). Implementing 2FA is just like including a excessive-tech alarm tool to complement the locks to your doorways.

Educating and Encouraging Users: If your internet site supports more than one customers, the significance of 2FA can not be overstated. Educate your clients approximately its significance and inspire its adoption. In a digital panorama rife with safety breaches, coaching your customers on the ones practices is corresponding to constructing a community watch software; genuinely all people performs a component in the collective protection.

Choosing Reputable Themes and Plugins: Selecting Safe Tools

The Art of Choosing: The WordPress environment is replete with problems and plugins, every offering a variety of functionalities. However, the selection of those equipment need to now not be based totally totally on functionality. Safety and popularity should be key concerns. Opt for assignment topics and plugins from well-known, dependable assets, just like the WordPress repository. Before set up, scrutinize individual opinions, scores, and replace frequency – those are telltale signs of the reliability and safety of the software program.

Keeping Up-to-date: Regular updates of your trouble topics and plugins are a important component of net website online protection. Developers regularly release updates to patch vulnerabilities and decorate capability. Neglecting the ones updates is corresponding to leaving your virtual home home home windows open; it invitations trouble.

Utilizing Security Plugins: Your Digital Guardians

Implementing Security Plugins: In the arena of WordPress, protection plugins are akin to having a devoted security organization. They offer a whole lot of functions from firewall protection and malware scanning to intrusion detection. Popular alternatives embody Wordfence, Sucuri, and iThemes Security.

Configuring for Optimal Protection: Installing a safety plugin is actually step one. Proper configuration to fit your specific net net page wishes is crucial. This would probable include putting in region firewalls, scheduling ordinary scans, and configuring protection alerts. If this seems daunting, preserve in thoughts searching for professional help to make sure gold widespread setup.

Ongoing Vigilance thru Monitoring: Most safety plugins offer monitoring services, presenting everyday reviews on the fitness and safety of your net page. Regular examine of those opinions is critical. It allows in early detection of potential threats, taking into consideration fast movement to mitigate any risks.

Incorporating those entire protection practices elevates the safety of your WordPress web web page, transforming it from a easy virtual presence to a fortified virtual fort. A robust internet website no longer awesome protects your hobbies but moreover fosters bear in mind among your visitors, growing a steady area for virtual interplay. Remember, within the realm of cybersecurity, vigilance and proactivity are your splendid allies. Stay in advance of threats and maintain a sturdy defense to make certain a constant on line enjoy for you and your clients.

Performance Optimization

In the digital age, the fee of your internet site is a critical element that influences now not wonderful character experience however moreover searching for engine rankings. A speedy and responsive net internet web page can notably decorate consumer delight, engagement, and conversion costs. In this advanced segment, we delve into complete techniques for optimizing your internet net page's overall performance, that specialize in 3 key areas: caching plugins, selecting the proper internet website hosting organization, and photograph optimization. Each of these elements performs a important characteristic in streamlining your internet site's operation, ensuring it runs smoothly and correctly.

Caching Plugins: Accelerating Your Site

The Power of Caching: Caching is a era that dramatically enhances your website's pace with the aid of manner of storing often accessed records in a quick retrievable layout. It lets in your net web website to serve up pages with out regenerating them from scratch each time a request is made. This technique appreciably reduces server load and internet page loading times, offering a smoother enjoy to your site visitors.

Selecting the Best Caching Plugins: The WordPress environment gives quite some caching plugins, each with precise talents and configurations. Choosing the proper plugin is essential. Opt for ones which is probably tremendously rated and preserve compatibility together collectively together with your model of WordPress. Some vital caching answers embody W3 Total Cache and WP Super Cache, known for his or her complete caching capabilities and customization alternatives.

Chapter 10: The Backbone Of Your Website

Understanding Hosting Options: The desire of web hosting has a profound impact in your website's usual standard overall performance. The essential forms of internet website hosting encompass shared, Virtual Private Server (VPS), dedicated, and managed Word Press internet hosting. Each kind gives unique degrees of belongings, safety, and manipulate. Shared website hosting is charge-effective but may additionally moreover lack usual performance, whilst VPS and devoted web hosting provide extra property and better control Managed WordPress website hosting offers optimized surroundings especially for Word Press internet websites, with talents like computerized updates and more potent protection.

Criteria for a Quality Host: When selecting an internet website hosting agency, prioritize basic performance and reliability. A host with rapid server reaction instances and immoderate uptime opportunities guarantees that your internet page is constantly available and responsive. Read evaluations, examine overall performance metrics, and in all likelihood take a look at the hosting provider in advance than making a very final choice.

Scalability for Growth: Choose an internet website hosting employer that gives scalability. As your internet web site grows in visitors and complexity, you may need to beautify your web website hosting plan. A top hosting provider must allow for easy scaling of sources to address your website on-line's growth with out inflicting downtime or simple overall overall performance troubles.

WordPress-Specific Features: Hosting providers that provide WordPress-specific functions can significantly simplify web page manage. Look for features like one-click on on on WordPress installs, automated updates, and specialised WordPress guide. These talents make certain that your internet website online is usually on foot the modern-day software application, this is crucial for every simple usual overall performance and safety.

Image Optimization: Balancing Quality and Performance

Resizing and Formatting Images: Large, excessive-desire images can dramatically sluggish down your net site. It's essential to resize your snap shots to the proper dimensions that they'll be exhibited to your internet net web page. Additionally, choosing the proper record format performs a vital function; JPEG is right for images because of its balance of fine and file period, at the same time as PNG is higher applicable for photos with transparency.

Utilizing Compression Tools: Image compression is a method that reduces document period with out noticeably sacrificing first-class. Tools and plugins like Smush and TinyPNG can automate this compression system. By reducing photo record sizes, you could considerably decrease page load times, enhancing the person enjoy.

Implementing Lazy Loading: Lazy loading is an optimization technique in which pix are loaded notable as they will be about to enter the viewport. This method that pictures at the bottom of the net web page aren't loaded till the consumer scrolls down. This technique can significantly lessen initial net web page load times, mainly for pages with a huge form of pix.

By meticulously enforcing the ones accepted universal overall performance optimization techniques, you could considerably beautify the rate and responsiveness of your WordPress internet site on-line. A faster internet internet website online not awesome delights your website visitors but moreover positions your net site favorably in seek engine ratings. Remember, within the speedy-paced digital global, tempo isn't always a steeply-priced, but a need for a a success online presence.

are trying to find engine advertising Optimization

Search Engine Optimization (search engine optimization) is a important manner for reinforcing your net web web page's visibility and making it without difficulty reachable to your target marketplace via engines like google like google and yahoo. Excelling in search engine marketing consequences in higher rankings in are seeking out outcomes, the usage of greater applicable internet site on-line site traffic in your internet web page. This advanced segment delves deeper into using seek engine advertising and marketing plugins, like Yoast seek engine advertising, and gives whole steerage on growing top notch content cloth fabric and getting to know search engine optimization fundamentals to seriously enhance your net website online's are searching for engine ranking.

Mastering seo Fundamentals

On-Page Optimization: On-internet internet web page search engine optimization factors like title tags, meta descriptions, header tags, and inner linking are essential. They are crucial for helping search engines understand the context and relevance of your content material material. Title tags and meta descriptions should be compelling and include primary key phrases. Header tags (H1, H2, H3, and so forth.) form your content material and make it more readable, every for clients and search engines like google like google. Internal linking improves internet internet web page navigation and allows distribute net page authority all through your internet internet site.

Mobile Optimization: With Google's cellular-first indexing, ensuring that your net internet site online is cellular-nice is greater essential than ever. This manner designing your internet website to be responsive, with speedy loading instances and easy navigation on cell gadgets. Google's Mobile-Friendly Test will let you test your net web web page's cell compatibility.

Page Speed Optimization: Page pace is a good sized detail in search engine optimization and customer experience. Faster loading web internet sites are desired via the use of search engines like google and customers alike. Utilize gadget like Google PageSpeed Insights to investigate and enhance your website's loading instances. Techniques collectively with minimizing CSS and JavaScript, optimizing pictures, and making use of caching can appreciably decorate pace.

Enhancing User Experience (UX): search engine marketing isn't just about key terms and again-hyperlinks; it's more and more about the general client revel in. This consists of intuitive internet site on-line navigation, a smooth and appealing layout, and content material material format. Websites that offer a higher customer experience have a tendency to rank higher in are seeking out consequences. Regularly accumulate customer feedback and use internet website analytics to recognize and improve the individual journey on your net web page on line.

Backup and Recovery

Regular backups are essential for the safety and integrity of any internet website on-line. They act as a safety net, safeguarding your net site toward information loss because of diverse surprising incidents like hacking, accidental deletions, or server failures. In this increased section, we are able to discover extensive the vital importance of a dependable backup device and manual you through the complete technique of backing up and restoring your WordPress internet site, making sure preparedness for any state of affairs.

The Importance of Regular Backups

Protection Against Data Loss: Regular backups are your first line of safety in the direction of information loss. They make certain you have got a present day duplicate of your internet web web page's content material, settings, and shape. This is particularly essential in times of information corruption or unintentional loss. Think of backups as coverage to your on line content fabric – vital for retaining the continuity of your virtual presence.

Recovery from Hacks: In the unfortunate occasion of a protection breach, having a clean backup is your fastest course to recuperation. It permits you to restore your net internet site to its country in advance than the hack, minimizing downtime and shortage of data. Regular backups are consequently crucial now not simplest for information safety, however additionally for preserving take delivery of as right with at the side of your clients.

Safeguard During Updates and Changes: Whenever you're making huge adjustments or updates in your web page, backups provide a vital fallback desire. If some component goes awry during the replace way, you could without trouble revert to a previous state, ensuring that your internet site stays beneficial and information isn't always misplaced.

Setting Up a Reliable Backup System

Selecting a Suitable Backup Solution: The WordPress surroundings gives severa backup solutions, each tailor-made to precise dreams and sizes of net internet web sites. Popular plugins like UpdraftPlus, BackupBuddy, and VaultPress provide sturdy backup abilities. When choosing a backup answer, hold in mind factors like ease of use, storage alternatives, and frequency of backups.

Automating Backup Processes: Automating your backup approach is top to ensuring ordinary and regular backups. Set your backup machine to run at regular intervals – every day, weekly, or month-to-month – relying on the frequency of your net internet page content cloth material updates. Automated backups make certain that the modern-day version of your internet site online is usually stored without requiring manual intervention.

Diverse Backup Storage: Storing your backups in more than one locations is important for ensuring their availability in any situation. This consists of storing backups for your website hosting server, cloud storage offerings like Dropbox or Google Drive, or even offline garage. This redundancy safeguards your backups in the direction of server failures, records corruption, or different unexpected incidents.

Restoring Your Website from a Backup

Understanding the Restoration Process: Familiarize yourself with the recovery way of your preferred backup solution. This expertise is essential to restoring your internet site online short and efficiently in case of an emergency. Each backup answer has a specific recovery technique, which ought to be understood and tested.

Testing Backups: Regularly attempting out your backups with the useful resource of restoring them in a staging surroundings is a extremely good exercise. This ensures that your backups are functioning effectively and which you are familiar with the restoration technique. It additionally permits pick out out any ability problems in the backup that might prevent a a success recovery.

Steps for Recovery: In the occasion which you want to repair your website on line, observe the precise steps provided via manner of your backup answer. This normally entails getting access to your backup storage, deciding on the favored backup, and beginning the repair system. Each step want to be observed cautiously to make sure a clean and complete healing of your internet site.

Post-Restoration Checks: After restoring your internet site, behavior an intensive test to make certain that each one functionalities and content cloth are accurate and going for walks as supposed. Verify that each one links are sensible, paperwork are filing correctly, and that no data has been out of place or corrupted within the machine.

By enforcing a robust backup and restoration gadget, you significantly mitigate the risk of irreparable statistics loss and ensure that your internet website on-line can speedy recover from any unforeseen incidents. Regular backups aren't best a habitual renovation undertaking; they'll be essential to the prolonged-term health and resilience of your online presence.

Chapter 11: Content Management

Effective content manipulate is the cornerstone of preserving a net website no longer only sparkling and up to date however additionally attractive and relevant for your target market. In this whole section, we delve into strategies for dealing with your internet web page's content material with finesse. We'll reputation on harnessing the overall capacity of the Elementor editor, correctly consisting of and optimizing media, and handling your posts and pages to keep your internet web site dynamic and charming.

Using Elementor Editor Effectively

Elementor's Interface: Elementor's purchaser-friendly drag-and-drop interface makes it easy to layout pages even as no longer having to jot down code. Familiarize yourself with its array of widgets, which provide functionalities starting from essential textual content improving to complex sliders.

Design and Layout: Elementor gives a plethora of layout options. Experiment with specific layouts, colour schemes, and typography to create pages that align together along with your emblem identification.

Responsive Design Considerations: One of Elementor's strengths is its responsive layout competencies. Utilize its mobile editing device to make sure your website on-line seems high-quality and capabilities properly on all gadgets, from desktops to smartphones.

Templates and Pre-Designed Blocks: Leverage Elementor's large library of pre-designed templates and blocks. These can be custom designed to suit your unique desires, offering a quick and green manner to layout new pages or refresh gift ones.

Interactive Elements: Explore Elementor's interactive elements like lively headlines and picture carousels. These functions could make your net internet site more engaging and visually attractive.

Efficiently Adding and Managing Media on Your Website

Effective Use of the Media Library: WordPress's Media Library is a powerful tool for handling photos, motion images, and other files. Regularly evaluation and easy your library to keep it prepared and make sure quick get entry to to media.

Image Optimization Techniques: Large picture files can gradual down your net website. Use system like Photoshop or on-line compressors to reduce report length with out compromising fine. Remember, quicker-loading pages provide a better character enjoy and make contributions to seo.

Accessibility and search engine optimization with Alt Text: Alt textual content is not most effective critical for seo but additionally for accessibility. Describe your snap shots because it ought to be just so display readers can interpret them for visually impaired customers.

Video and Audio Content: When incorporating video or audio, host massive files externally (e.G., YouTube, Vimeo) to avoid straining your server. Ensure all multimedia is responsive and available.

Managing Posts and Pages

Regular Content Updates: Keep a content cloth material calendar to plot and execute everyday updates. This must consist of latest weblog posts, updating present content material, or removing antique material.

Utilizing Categories and Tags: Categories and tags are crucial for organizing content material fabric and helping customers discover relevant information fast. Use instructions to extensively organisation posts and tags to give an explanation for unique facts.

search engine marketing-Friendly Content: Ensure your content material is optimized for serps like google. This consists of the usage of centered key phrases, growing attractive meta titles and descriptions, and structuring content material material with headers for higher readability.

Content Archiving Strategies: Not all content material material cloth remains applicable indefinitely. Develop a method for archiving vintage posts, that may include updating them with new data, redirecting to more current content material material, or casting off them if now not applicable.

Feedback and Engagement: Encourage man or woman engagement by using which consist of statement sections and feedback paperwork. Regularly examine character remarks to gain insights and foster a network spherical your content material.

Content Analysis: Use analytics equipment to song which content cloth cloth performs well. Analyzing metrics which includes net internet web page views, time spent on net web page, and bounce fee can offer precious insights into target market selections and content effectiveness.

By learning these content material fabric control techniques, your net website on-line will now not simplest trap site traffic however moreover preserve them engaged and returning. High-great, nicely-controlled content material shows undoubtedly in your emblem, enhances customer experience, and contributes considerably to the achievement of your internet web site.

Plugin Management

WordPress plugins play a pivotal function in enhancing your net site's functionality and abilities. The massive array of plugins to be had can be each a boon and a assignment. With such loads of alternatives, selecting and effectively coping with the proper plugins is critical for ensuring maximum superb common performance and protection of your internet website online. In this expanded segment, we dive deeper into techniques for choosing the exceptional plugins to fulfill your unique wishes and maintaining them correctly to make sure your net web page runs without difficulty and securely.

Choosing the Right Plugins: A Strategic Approach

Identifying Specific Needs: The first step in plugin preference is a clean knowledge of what you need the plugins to benefit. Your necessities might in all likelihood variety from boosting seo, accelerating net site tempo, to which include customer engagement capabilities like contact paperwork or social media integration. Defining your desires gadgets a smooth path for the sorts of plugins you want to be seeking out.

In-Depth Research and Reviews: Once your needs are defined, embark on thorough research to discover plugins that align collectively along with your requirements. Delve into client reviews, take a look at plugin scores, and do not forget the variety of lively installations. This studies affords treasured insights into the plugin’s reliability, client experience, and stylish effectiveness. Be conscious of the developer's recognition and the plugin's update data as those elements frequently mean its reliability and sturdiness.

Ensuring Compatibility and Regular Updates: Compatibility at the side of your contemporary WordPress model is non-negotiable. Additionally, prioritize plugins that benefit everyday updates from their developers. Regular updates commonly deal with safety vulnerabilities, introduce new competencies, and make certain compatibility with the cutting-edge WordPress version, that is essential for retaining a constant and green net website on-line.

Testing Before Full Integration: If feasible, conduct tests in a staging surroundings earlier than genuinely integrating a plugin into your live net page. This attempting out segment permits you to assess the plugin's capability and its impact for your internet site on-line's regular performance without risking your stay surroundings. This step is especially important for complicated plugins or those who notably adjust your internet website online's functionality.

Chapter 12: Ensuring Peak Performance

Commitment to Regular Updates: Diligently preserve your plugins updated. Updates are not pretty much new features; they often include vital safety patches and common performance upgrades. Neglecting updates can depart your internet website on line susceptible to protection breaches and compatibility issues.

Monitoring Plugin Performance: Regularly display how each plugin influences your website Some plugins, mainly useful resource-intensive ones, can significantly gradual down your internet internet site. Keep song of your website online's loading instances and normal performance. If a plugin is adversely affecting performance, don't forget possibility solutions.

Pruning Unnecessary Plugins: A cluttered plugin library may be a liability. Regularly evaluation and cast off any plugins which is probably now not vital. This workout not simplest reduces functionality protection risks however additionally allows in preserving a purifier, more green WordPress environment.

Safeguarding with Backups: Always again up your internet web page earlier than imposing any plugin updates. This precautionary step is your protection internet, permitting you to rapid repair your net site online to its previous kingdom if an update causes troubles.

Security First: Avoiding Risks: Be cautious of nulled or pirated plugins, as they may be frequently property of malicious code. Always source your plugins from respectable structures much like the WordPress Plugin Directory or at once from relied on developers' net websites. This workout guarantees that you are the usage of secure, regular, and jail software program to your internet internet web page.

By adhering to these complete plugin manipulate techniques, you may appreciably enhance the capability and protection of your WordPress web internet page. Effective plugin manage is prepared placing the right balance - it is approximately choosing plugins that add massive fee on your net site on line whilst maintaining a lean, steady, and immoderate-acting digital surroundings. Remember, inside the global of WordPress plugins, excellent and strategic preference regularly outweigh quantity.

Website Analytics

Understanding your purpose marketplace and analyzing your internet web page web web page visitors are vital for the boom and refinement of your on line presence. Website analytics offer a treasure trove of insights into patron behavior, internet site on line site visitors sources, and content material cloth material common overall performance. In this prolonged segment, we delve into the nuances of integrating system like Google Analytics into your WordPress net internet page. We additionally find out how to interpret key metrics efficiently to make informed alternatives that foster growth and non-save you improvement.

Integrating Google Analytics for Comprehensive Insights

Setting Up Google Analytics: To start harnessing the power of analytics, first set up a Google Analytics account. Once finished, add your internet internet website as a assets inner your Analytics account, which generates a completely precise tracking code. This code is the gateway to unlocking a wealth of records about your net web site's website online visitors and man or woman interactions.

Effortless Plugin Integration: WordPress offers various plugins like MonsterInsights or Analytify that simplify the integration of Google Analytics. These plugins allow seamless connection of your Google Analytics account together with your WordPress net web site, bypassing the need for guide code enhancing. They offer individual-great interfaces and further features like dashboard analytics evaluations, making it much less complex to access and recognize your data.

Manual Code Insertion for Advanced Control: For folks that opt for a more direct technique, manually putting the Google Analytics monitoring code into your net web page's header is an opportunity. This can be carried out through your subject matter's settings or via manner of the usage of improving the header.Php report. This approach gives more manage and can be favored by means of manner of humans with technical expertise.

Interpreting Key Metrics for Informed Decision Making

Analyzing Traffic Sources: Understanding wherein your traffic originate – be it search engines like google like google, social media, or direct visits – is top in identifying powerful advertising strategies. This analysis enables in allocating belongings to the channels that yield the maximum traffic and engagement.

User Behavior Insights: Metrics like net internet web page perspectives, jump fee, and common session period offer a window into how customers interact collectively together along with your internet site online. These insights are useful in shaping content material fabric approach and making web site design enhancements. They assist in know-how what captures patron hobby and encourages longer net internet site visits.

Content Performance Evaluation: Identifying which pages and posts garner the most interest and engagement permits in tailoring your content material cloth method. By information what resonates together along with your purpose market, you can produce extra of the content material fabric fabric that drives visitors and engagement.

Conversion Tracking for ROI Analysis: For internet websites with precise goals along with shape submissions, e-trade sales, or e-e-newsletter sign-ups, tracking these conversions is important. Google Analytics lets in you to song these moves, offering insights into the effectiveness of your calls-to-motion and the general go back on investment (ROI) of your advertising and advertising and marketing efforts.

Understanding Audience Demographics: Delving into the demographics of your audience – which embody age, gender, and pastimes – allows for added centered and effective content cloth material and advertising and advertising and marketing strategies. This tailor-made method can appreciably beautify customer engagement and conversion fees.

Regular Review and Adaptation for Ongoing Improvement

Consistent Analytics Review: Regularly reviewing your net website online analytics is important to live updated for your net page's standard typical performance and growing man or woman developments. This ongoing analysis lets in in figuring out areas for development and in adapting strategies to changing person behaviors and marketplace dynamics.

Strategic Adaptation Based on Insights: Utilize the insights received from analytics to constantly refine your advertising and marketing, search engine optimization, and content material material material material strategies. By being statistics-pushed on your technique, you could make changes which are more likely to yield fantastic results and boom.

Staying Informed and Evolving: The state of affairs of net analytics is dynamic, with new capabilities and extremely good practices rising often. Staying informed about the fashionable tendencies in device like Google Analytics guarantees that you are leveraging the general capacity of those structures to your website's benefit.

By correctly integrating and using internet site analytics, you gain essential insights that power informed selection-making. This know-how of your goal market and their interactions together together with your website online is instrumental in improving the consumer revel in, growing website site visitors, and contributing extensively to the achievement and increase of your internet web page.

Mobile Responsiveness

In modern virtual panorama, in which cell gadgets regularly outpace computer systems in net usage, having a internet website online this is responsive isn't always simply useful—

it is crucial. Responsive net layout ensures that your website offers a unbroken, maximum exceptional viewing experience throughout masses of gadgets, adapting to super show screen sizes without sacrificing functionality or aesthetics. This extended phase delves into the critical importance of responsive design and gives precise guidance to make certain that your WordPress internet page is absolutely optimized for mobile responsiveness.

Understanding the Essentials of Responsive Design

The Core Principle of Responsive Design: At its coronary coronary heart, responsive layout way that your internet website's layout and content fluidly alter to healthy the display screen length on which it is appeared. This dynamic adaptability is important not only for consumer revel in however also for seek engine advertising. Responsive design eradicates the need for separate cellular web websites, streamlining content material cloth material manipulate and ensuring a ordinary emblem experience at some point of all structures.

search engine optimization Benefits of Mobile-Friendly Design: In the sector of search engine advertising, mobile-friendliness is a crucial hassle. Google and one among a kind primary serps like google like google prioritize cellular-optimized web sites in their rankings, mainly with the appearance of cellular-first indexing. A responsive internet site stands a better chance of sporting out better rankings in are looking for results, tapping into the large cell man or woman base.

Enhancing User Experience (UX): A responsive website on-line significantly enhances client revel in through imparting a ordinary and available interface regardless of the device used. This adaptability ends in lower leap charges and better engagement and conversion costs, as users revel in a problem-unfastened browsing experience.

Strategies to Ensure Your Site is Responsive

Selecting the Right Responsive Themes: Begin through the use of the usage of selecting a WordPress subject matter that inherently enables responsive layout. WordPress gives a massive choice of situation matters which is probably crafted to be cell-first-rate, ensuring that their format and functionality adapt seamlessly throughout one-of-a-kind devices. When selecting a topic, make certain it's far designed to be responsive and test it at some stage in a couple of devices for consistency.

Comprehensive Device Testing: Regularly test your website's look and functionality on diverse gadgets, which consist of each smartphones and pills. Utilize gear like Google’s Mobile-Friendly Test to evaluate how well your internet web site online plays on awesome monitors. This attempting out allows pick out and rectify any responsiveness problems, ensuring a universally smooth man or woman revel in.

Optimization of Images and Media: Optimizing photos and media for responsive layout is essential. Ensure that your visual content material fabric material is adaptable, with pictures and movies that resize accurately to in form super show show display resolutions and sizes without dropping clarity or first-rate. This method facilitates in retaining speedy loading times and an aesthetically attractive format on all devices.

Responsive Navigation and Menus: Navigation is a key problem of customer experience. Focus on developing menus and navigation elements which might be without issues to be had and client-high-quality on smaller monitors. Dropdowns, hamburger menus, and contact-satisfactory interfaces can substantially decorate navigation on cellular devices.

Chapter 13: Implementing Responsive Design Best Practices

Utilizing Fluid Grids: Employ fluid grid layouts that use relative devices, collectively with opportunities, in desire to fixed devices like pixels. Fluid grids permit for content fabric and factors to resize and adjust based on the display length, contributing to a simply responsive layout.

Flexible Images for Seamless Display: Implement bendy photos that automatically resize interior their field factors. This approach guarantees images do now not amplify beyond the display display width, preserving the integrity of your layout on numerous gadgets.

Employing CSS Media Queries: CSS media queries are a cornerstone of responsive layout. They will let you use wonderful styling pointers for your internet website on-line primarily based at the tool's show screen duration, selection, and orientation, bearing in mind tailor-made displays on severa devices.

Creating Touch-Friendly Interfaces: In a mobile-ruled global, ensuring that interactive factors like buttons and hyperlinks are contact-first-class is essential. Adequate period and spacing for those factors are essential to provide a snug and intuitive contact experience.

By embracing and effectively implementing responsive format, you ensure that your internet website isn't most effective available however additionally gives a captivating and fulfilling experience for clients in the course of all devices. It transcends mere version to smaller displays; it's far about crafting a internet website online it's far intuitively navigable and aesthetically lovely, no matter how it's miles accessed.

Legal Compliance

Adhering to jail requirements much like the General Data Protection Regulation (GDPR) and distinct nearby legal tips is a essential duty for internet web page owners. Non-compliance risks now not fine substantial financial outcomes however moreover excessive damage for your popularity. In this accelerated phase, we delve deeper into statistics the important difficulty prison requirements important for net internet site on-line operation and pressure the importance of consulting with legal experts to make certain that your website meets all essential jail requirements.

Understanding and Meeting Legal Requirements

Data Protection and Privacy Laws: Laws which includes the GDPR are designed to defend the non-public information of humans, especially inside the European Union. However, the gain of GDPR extends beyond EU borders. If your net web website dreams or collects records from EU residents, compliance is obligatory irrespective of in which your net website on line is based totally. This includes statistics the way to cope with character statistics, from series to garage and processing.

Cookie Policy Compliance: Many regions spherical the area now require net web sites to inform web page visitors about the use of cookies, specifically those used for monitoring and analytics. This consists of not simply notifying traffic but moreover acquiring their consent. Understanding and imposing the ones necessities is crucial for crook compliance, as well as for keeping transparency and keep in mind collectively at the side of your clients.

Web Accessibility and Inclusivity: Ensuring your internet website is obtainable to all clients, which embody human beings with disabilities, isn't always just a pleasing workout however additionally a criminal requirement in lots of regions. Compliance with requirements just like the Web Content Accessibility Guidelines (WCAG) is important. These tips assist make the internet more available to people with numerous disabilities, along with visual, auditory, physical, speech, cognitive, language, learning, and neurological disabilities.

The Role of Legal Experts in Ensuring Compliance

Seeking Expert Legal Advice: Given the complexity and versions of net prison pointers throughout considered one of a kind areas, consulting with criminal experts who focus on on-line and statistics safety prison suggestions is specifically beneficial. These professionals can provide the important guidance to navigate the complicated prison panorama, supporting you avoid commonplace pitfalls.

Customizing Legal Documents: Tailored prison documents like terms of provider, privateness regulations, and cookie consent paperwork are essential for compliance. Legal professionals can assist draft the ones files to mirror the precise operations of your internet site and the man or woman of your person base, making sure they're whole and compliant with current criminal guidelines.

Staying Updated with Legal Changes: Legal requirements are ever-evolving. Regular consultations with criminal professionals can keep you informed approximately new legal guidelines, amendments, and interpretations that might impact your internet internet site online. Staying current-day is essential for ongoing compliance.

Implementing Compliance Measures Effectively

Displaying a Clear Privacy Policy: Your internet site should function a clear and entire privateness insurance that outlines how to procure, use, keep, and protect person statistics. This transparency isn't only a prison requirement but additionally fosters receive as authentic with and credibility in conjunction with your internet website on-line traffic.

Cookie Consent Mechanisms: If your internet website online uses cookies, specially for tracking and analytics, imposing a cookie consent mechanism is vital. This system ought to provide clear information and an smooth way for customers to provide or withdraw consent.

Conducting Regular Compliance Audits: Regular audits of your net internet site are crucial to make sure ongoing compliance with relevant legal tips and policies. These audits can help pick out regions wherein your net website on line can also fall brief of criminal requirements, bearing in mind nicely timed rectifications.

By placing a immoderate precedence on prison compliance, you guard your net website from capacity criminal problems and construct a foundation of agree with together along with your web site traffic. Demonstrating a dedication to privacy, safety, and accessibility now not only enhances your net web web page's reputation but moreover fosters a more inclusive and respectful on-line environment.

Chapter 14: Word Press As A Money-Making Platform

In the virtual age, the internet has spread out exceptional opportunities for people and companies alike to generate income on line. One of the simplest and on hand avenues for achieving this is thru the use of WordPress—a flexible and client-first-rate content fabric manage tool that has end up synonymous with internet publishing and on line presence manipulate.

This chapter serves as an creation to the concept of utilizing WordPress as a sturdy platform for economic advantage. It seeks to provide readers with a foundational statistics of WordPress and its intrinsic capacity as a rewarding device. By the forestall of this financial catastrophe, you will have received perception into the following key regions:

Understanding WordPress as a Versatile Content Management System: WordPress, at the beginning conceived as a running a weblog platform, has superior right proper right into a multifaceted content material manage gadget able to assisting a severa form of net web site kinds. We will delve into the historical evolution of WordPress and its pivotal function in shaping the current net.

Why WordPress Is an Ideal Platform for Earning Money Online: We will find out the high-quality blessings that WordPress offers to the ones aspiring to generate profits via online ventures. These blessings encompass its accessibility, scalability, customization talents, and a colorful

environment of plugins and themes.

Setting Your Financial Goals and Expectations: Before embarking on your WordPress journey, it's miles vital to establish easy economic goals and manipulate your expectations. We will manual you via the way of defining your financial goals, considering severa monetization strategies and potential profits streams.

Building the Foundation: Creating Your WordPress Website

Your journey towards monetizing your WordPress internet website begins offevolved with building a sturdy foundation. In this bankruptcy, we're able to explore the important steps required to set up your on-line presence correctly. By the surrender of this chapter, you could have gained insights into the subsequent key areas:

Choosing a Niche and Target Audience: Selecting the proper location of interest is a essential choice that shapes the route and success of your WordPress internet net site. We will talk strategies for figuring out niches that align in conjunction with your pastimes, records, and market demand. Additionally, we can delve into expertise your target audience to tailor your content material and offerings therefore.

Selecting a Domain Name and Hosting Provider: Your domain call is your virtual deal with, and your internet web hosting organisation is the foundation upon which your website is built. We will guide you through the process of selecting a internet site name this is memorable, relevant, and brandable. You'll moreover learn how to choose out a reliable internet web hosting company to ensure your net website online's balance and overall performance.

Installing WordPress and Basic Website Setup: Setting up WordPress can also seem daunting, but it is a sincere system with step-by manner of-step steering. We'll stroll you through the installation device, together with configuring vital settings, choosing a topic, and putting in crucial plugins. By the give up of this segment, your WordPress internet site can be organized to take shape.

Crafting Quality Content

Content is the lifeblood of your WordPress internet web site, and it plays a pivotal function in attracting and preserving traffic. In this financial catastrophe, we're capable of dive deep into the art of creating content material that resonates along side your target market and maintains them coming lower lower back for added. By the forestall of this financial ruin, you will have honed your abilties within the following key areas:

The Importance of High-Quality Content: Quality is paramount within the virtual realm. We will talk why developing extremely good content material material cloth is nonnegotiable and discover the blessings it brings, which consist of advanced search engine ratings, elevated engagement, and additional suitable credibility.

Writing Engaging Blog Posts and Articles: Whether you are a seasoned writer or honestly starting, this phase will provide realistic tips on crafting weblog posts and articles that captivate your readers. We'll communicate writing strategies, structuring your content material fabric fabric for clarity, and optimizing it for engines like google like google.

Creating Multimedia Content: Videos, Podcasts, and More: Diversifying your content fabric portfolio can significantly make bigger your achieve and engagement. We'll discover the area of multimedia content material, consisting of video introduction, podcasting, and visible storytelling. You'll benefit insights into device and strategies for producing compelling multimedia content material.

Effective Content Planning and Scheduling: Consistency is essential as regards to content material creation. We'll introduce you to content fabric cloth planning and scheduling strategies that will help you maintain a everyday publishing cadence. This ensures that your target audience remains engaged and informed.

As you improvement thru those chapters, hold in thoughts that building a a success WordPress internet web web page is an iterative device. By studying the foundational components of niche preference, net site setup, and content creation, you will be well on your manner to developing a platform that not simplest draws web site traffic however additionally gadgets the degree for numerous monetization techniques explored in next chapters.

Optimizing for Search Engines (are looking for engine marketing and advertising)

In the virtual landscape, visibility is paramount, and accomplishing excessive are trying to find engine rankings can substantially effect the fulfillment of your WordPress net website. Search Engine Optimization (search engine optimization) is the artwork and technological knowledge of improving your internet website's on line presence. In this financial ruin, we're capable of delve into the intricacies of seek engine marketing, providing you with the know-how and tools to boost your net net site's visibility and herbal traffic. By the quit of this financial disaster, you can have acquired understanding inside the following key regions:

seo Fundamentals and Its Role in Online Success: Understanding the important standards of seo is vital. We will find out how engines like google like google and yahoo art work, the importance of key phrases, and the factors which have an effect on are trying to find engine scores. You might also even preserve near why seo is crucial for your online success.

Keyword Research and On-Page seo

Techniques: Keyword research is the muse of powerful seek engine advertising and marketing. We will manual you thru the way of identifying relevant keywords, assessing opposition, and strategically incorporating them into your content material material. You will even examine onepage seo strategies, which includes optimizing titles, Meta descriptions, and headings for search engines.

Off-Page seo Strategies and Link Building: Offpage searching for engine advertising is set building your internet site's authority and popularity in the digital panorama. We will communicate the significance of one manner links and delve into ethical hyperlink-constructing strategies that can enhance your internet website on-line's credibility and seek engine ratings.

Monitoring are trying to find engine advertising Progress and Results. search engine marketing is an ongoing technique, and monitoring your efforts is vital. We will introduce you to gear and metrics for monitoring your seek engine advertising and marketing everyday overall performance, collectively with organic website online site visitors, key-word scores, and purchaser engagement. You'll learn how to interpret information and make knowledgeable adjustments in your seo technique.

By gaining knowledge of the thoughts of are seeking engine advertising and advertising, you may equip your WordPress internet web page with the functionality to rank better in are attempting to find engine outcomes, lure more herbal net web page visitors, and create a strong foundation for diverse monetization strategies explored in later chapters. Remember that seek engine marketing is an prolonged-time period funding, and your dedication to ongoing optimization will yield big rewards inside the aggressive on-line panorama.

Chapter 15: Monetization Strategies

The number one intention of many Word Press internet site proprietors is to turn their passion and information proper right into a sustainable supply of profits. In this financial disaster, we are able to discover numerous monetization techniques that can transform your internet site from a digital presence right right into a sales-producing asset. By the give up of this financial wreck, you may have a entire

statistics of the subsequent key monetization strategies:

Understanding the Various Ways to Make Money with Your WordPress Website: Monetization is not a one-size-fits-all endeavor. We will introduce you to severa strategies of producing income on-line and help you find out which strategies align together along with your internet internet site's location of interest, goal market, and dreams.

Displaying Ads: Google AdSense and Beyond: Advertising is a ubiquitous revenue flow into for online content material cloth cloth creators. We will speak a manner to integrate advertising, which includes Google AdSense and opportunity advert networks, into your website successfully. You'll have a look at ad placement, ad kinds, and optimizing ad sales.

Affiliate Marketing: Promoting Products and Earning Commissions: Affiliate marketing and advertising and advertising is a effective manner to monetize your internet website via way of promoting products or services relevant on your place of hobby. We'll manual you via the intricacies of affiliate marketing and advertising and marketing and marketing, from deciding on accomplice programs to crafting compelling product pointers.

Selling Digital and Physical Products: If you have got had been given facts or products to offer, your WordPress net website online can characteristic a rewarding e-commerce platform. We will discover the technique of putting in area a web keep, inclusive of product preference, pricing, rate gateways, and achievement.

Membership Sites and Subscription-Based Content: Monetizing your expertise or top rate content material cloth through membership websites and subscription fashions can offer a routine deliver of earnings. We will speak techniques for growing surely one in all a kind content material fabric, dealing with memberships, and nurturing a faithful subscriber base.

Each monetization technique has its unique strengths and issues. By the surrender of this bankruptcy, you may be prepared with the expertise and insights had to make knowledgeable alternatives approximately which techniques align collectively alongside your internet site on line's niche, audience, and long-time period dreams. Remember that diversifying your profits streams can beautify financial stability and resilience inside the dynamic worldwide of on-line entrepreneurship.

Leveraging Email Marketing

In the virtual landscape, building and nurturing relationships along with your target market is crucial for lengthy-time period success. Email advertising is a effective tool that lets in you to have interaction along with your goal market, supply valuable content, and strength earnings. In this financial catastrophe, we are able to delve into the location of electronic mail advertising and marketing, presenting you with strategies and techniques to harness its functionality correctly. By the give up of this bankruptcy, you may have won statistics within the following key regions:

Building and Nurturing Your Email List: Your e-mail list is a treasured asset in your WordPress internet internet site on line. We will talk strategies for growing your subscriber base, consisting of pick-in paperwork, lead magnets, and incentives. You'll discover ways to maintain a clean and engaged electronic mail listing.

Crafting Effective Email Campaigns: Creating compelling e-mail campaigns is important for engaging your subscribers. We will find out the factors of a achievement electronic mail campaigns, collectively with trouble lInes, content material cloth shape, and calls to motion. You'll additionally discover incredible practices for

personalization and segmentation.

Automation and Segmentation for Better Results: Automation can streamline your e mail advertising efforts and supply customized content material in your subscribers. We will introduce you to e-mail advertising and marketing and marketing automation tools and reveal the way to apply segmentation to tailor your messages to unique audience segments.

Measuring the Success of Email Marketing: Data and analytics play a critical role in optimizing your e-mail advertising method. We will guide you through key e mail advertising and marketing and advertising and marketing metrics, which includes open expenses, click on on-through prices, and conversion prices. You'll discover ways to interpret the ones metrics and make information-driven improvements.

Email advertising and advertising is a flexible tool that could beautify individual engagement, promote services or products, and generate sales. By reading the techniques and strategies supplied in this financial wreck, you'll be nicely-prepared to leverage email advertising and advertising as a valuable element of your WordPress internet site's monetization method. Remember that effective verbal exchange and relationship-constructing through email can reason a devoted and lively target market, fostering extended-time period success.

Social Media Marketing

In an era marked with the useful resource of world connectivity and social interplay, leveraging social media systems is a pivotal aspect of selling your WordPress net website and attractive collectively with your purpose market. In this bankruptcy, we will find out the strategies and exquisite practices of social media advertising and marketing to expand your online presence and reach. By the surrender of this chapter, you may have a complete

statistics of the subsequent key regions:

Utilizing Social Media Platforms to Promote Your Website: Social media structures offer a dynamic stage to reveal case your content material fabric and connect with your goal market. We will discuss the significance of various social media structures and the manner to pick out out the ones most applicable to your area of hobby and audience.

Developing a Social Media Strategy: Effective social media advertising starts offevolved

offevolved with a nicely-described technique. We will guide you through the manner of making a social media approach that aligns together together with your internet web website online's dreams, content material calendar, and target audience engagement goals.

Engaging with Your Audience and Building a Community: Building a devoted and interactive network around your brand is critical. We will discover techniques for enticing together along with your target marketplace authentically, responding to feedback, and fostering meaningful conversations.

Analytics and Performance Tracking: Measuring the impact of your social media efforts is crucial for refining your method. We will introduce you to social media analytics equipment and key performance signs and signs and symptoms (KPIs) to evaluate the effectiveness of your social media advertising campaigns.

In an ever-evolving digital panorama, social media advertising serves as a dynamic and influential channel for using net web site website traffic for your WordPress net website on-line, constructing brand attention, and nurturing your on-line network. By studying the strategies and techniques provided on this financial ruin, you will be properly-organized to harness the strength of social media to benefit your net web web site's goals and enhance its contemporary achievement. Remember that social media advertising is a non-prevent approach that evolves along technology and consumer alternatives, requiring adaptability and innovation to live relevant and powerful.

Chapter 16: Creating A Brand And Building Trust

In the virtual realm, keep in mind and credibility are foreign cash. Establishing a sturdy on line brand identity and building take delivery of as actual with at the side of your audience are vital for extended-term achievement. In this financial ruin, we're able to find out the intricacies of making a logo, nurturing agree with, and improving your website's consumer enjoy. By the stop of this chapter, you can have obtained know-how in the following key areas:

Establishing Your Online Brand Identity: Your emblem is extra than best a emblem; it represents your internet website online's man or woman and values. We will delve into the factors of logo identification, together with brand messaging, seen format, and tone of voice. You'll learn how to create a cohesive and remarkable emblem that resonates at the aspect of your target audience.

Building Trust and Credibility: Trust is the foundation of any a success on-line venture. We will speak strategies for setting up remember collectively along with your target market, which encompass transparency, consistency, and turning in on guarantees. You'll additionally discover ways to leverage social evidence, which includes testimonials and critiques, to decorate your internet site's credibility.

The Importance of User Experience and Website Design: User enjoy (UX) performs a essential characteristic in maintaining web site traffic and changing them into reliable customers or clients. We will discover UX fantastic practices, in conjunction with internet website navigation, mobile optimization, and responsive layout. You'll discover how a nicely-designed internet site can decorate user satisfaction and keep in mind.

Leveraging Testimonials and Reviews: Positive testimonials and critiques can notably have an effect on a traveller's desire to interact alongside side your net web page or make a purchase. We will speak techniques for collecting and showcasing testimonials and evaluations efficiently. You'll discover ways to leverage person-generated content to assemble credibility.

By that specialize in logo identification, take into account-building, and person experience, you can supply a lift to your WordPress net website's popularity and characteristic it for prolonged-term increase and success. Remember that building trust is an ongoing approach, and consistency and authenticity are key to preserving and

Analyzing and Optimizing Website Performance

Your WordPress internet internet site on-line's regular usual overall performance and patron experience are paramount to its fulfillment. In this bankruptcy, we're able to explore the gear and strategies essential to analyze, decorate, and optimize your net website on-line's performance, ensuring it remains competitive within the virtual panorama. By the surrender of this bankruptcy, you'll have acquired knowledge in the following key regions:

Using Google Analytics and Other Tools to Track Website Performance: Data-pushed decisionmaking is critical for enhancing your net net website's standard overall performance. We will introduce you to internet analytics device, with a focal point on Google Analytics, and manual you through the way of installing monitoring, monitoring key metrics, and deriving actionable insights.

Identifying Areas for Improvement: A critical step in optimizing your net internet web page is identifying regions that need improvement. We will talk techniques for wearing out net website online audits, which encompass

ordinary overall performance audits, content fabric audits and person enjoy tests. You'll learn how to pinpoint problems that may be hindering your net internet site on line's achievement.

Website Speed and Mobile Optimization: Fastloading net internet web sites are desired with the useful resource of each customers and search engines like google. We will discover the importance of internet site pace and cell optimization, presenting realistic hints and gadget to enhance your net web site's usual performance on diverse gadgets.

A/B Testing and Conversion Rate Optimization (CRO): Improving your net web page's conversion charge—whether or not or now not it's far for signal-ups, purchases, or different favored moves—is pinnacle to developing its

effectiveness. We will delve into A/B checking out and conversion price optimization strategies, supporting you behavior experiments and make facts-sponsored improvements.

Website overall performance optimization is an ongoing way that right now impacts client pride, seek engine ratings, and your website's customary fulfillment. By mastering the strategies and tools furnished on this financial ruin, you'll be wellequipped to investigate and optimize your WordPress internet web page, ensuring it continues to meet the evolving expectations of your goal market. Remember that internet internet page optimization isn't a one-time attempt but a non-stop willpower to offering an

Extremely good character experience.

Chapter 17: Scaling Your Word Press Business

As your Word Press internet website online profits traction and generates sales, the possibility for boom and enlargement will become an increasing number of feasible. This bankruptcy explores techniques and considerations for scaling your Word Press organization, taking it to the subsequent degree. By the surrender of this financial disaster, you may have an entire expertise of the subsequent key regions:

Expanding Your Website and Content Offerings: Diversification is a key driving stress of growth. We will speak strategies for increasing your internet site via manner of which incorporates new content material categories, offerings, or merchandise. You'll discover ways to understand possibilities for increase inside your location of hobby.

Outsourcing and Team Building: As your Word Press business company grows, you can discover it useful to enlist the assist of others.

We will discover the technique of outsourcing responsibilities and constructing a set, whether or now not or not via freelancers, contractors, or whole-time personnel. You'll find out a manner to delegate obligations and attention on strategic choice-making.

Diversifying Income Streams: Relying on a unmarried profits supply can be risky. We will communicate strategies for diversifying your income streams, which consist of exploring new monetization techniques, partner partnerships, and collaborations. You'll discover ways to create a greater resilient earnings version.

Preparing for the Future and Staying Updated: The digital land scape is ever-evolving. We will emphasize the significance of staying knowledgeable approximately enterprise inclinations, growing era, and changes in client conduct. You'll find out a way to adapt your WordPress business company to remain relevant and aggressive.

Scaling your WordPress commercial enterprise is a natural development that could free up new opportunities and growth your sales capability. By embracing growth techniques and staying attuned to the changing panorama, you can ensure the sustainability and prosperity of your WordPress project. Remember that scalability entails strategic planning and a commitment to

non-forestall development and innovation.

Legal and Ethical Considerations

Operating a WordPress internet site as a manner of manufacturing earnings consists of severa felony and ethical obligations. In this chapter, we will find out the prison and ethical issues that internet net page owners ought to navigate to make sure compliance, guard their customers, and uphold their reputation. By the give up of this chapter, you can have a complete facts of the following key regions:

Understanding Copyright and Intellectual Property: Intellectual belongings is a crucial factor of online content advent. We will delve into copyright regulation, honest use, and Creative Commons licenses. You'll discover ways to respect others' intellectual property rights at the same time as shielding your very personal.

Privacy Policies and GDPR Compliance: User privacy is a paramount hassle. We will talk the importance of having a privacy coverage in your internet internet site on line and find out the requirements of statistics safety policies along with the General Data Protection Regulation (GDPR). You'll find out a way to manage patron statistics responsibly.

Taxation and Financial Regulations: Generating income out of your internet web page can also furthermore have tax

implications. We will discover the economic and tax issues of on-line entrepreneurship, including profits reporting, tax deductions, and compliance with relevant tax criminal hints.

Ethical Considerations in Online Business: Maintaining ethical behavior is important for building take delivery of as actual with along side your target market and pals. We will communicate moral issues in regions consisting of associate marketing and advertising, product promotions, and sponsored content material material material. You'll discover ways to strike a balance among monetization and moral integrity.

Navigating the jail and moral panorama of on line entrepreneurship is important for protective your enterprise and reputation. By getting to know the necessities and practices provided in this financial disaster, you can make certain that your WordPress net internet site on-line operates in a accountable, compliant, and moral way. Remember that upholding jail and moral requirements no longer most effective safeguards your pastimes however moreover fosters do not forget and credibility collectively together with your intention marketplace.

Case Studies and Success Stories

Learning from actual-worldwide examples can provide valuable insights and concept on your WordPress adventure. In this financial damage, we can find out a collection of case research and achievement testimonies from humans and companies which have harnessed the energy of WordPress to reap first-rate results. By the surrender of this bankruptcy, you may advantage belief and practical insights into the following key regions:

Real-World Examples of Successful WordPress Website Owners: We will show off a numerous style of WordPress website proprietors, from bloggers and content material cloth creators to e-change marketers and place of hobby specialists. You'll discover about their unique journeys, stressful conditions they confronted, and strategies they employed to attain fulfillment.

Lessons Learned and Key Takeaways: Each case have a take a look at may be observed with the aid of way of a set of key take aways, distilling the vital classes and strategies that contributed to their achievement. You'll find out actionable insights that you could observe on your very private WordPress undertaking.

Adapting Strategies to Your Unique Context: While case studies offer treasured commands, it is critical to comply techniques on your net web site's region of interest, desires, and aim marketplace. We will talk a manner to draw concept from the ones fulfillment testimonies on the identical time as tailoring your approach on your precise conditions.

By delving into the reviews of others who've navigated the WordPress landscape efficiently, you'll advantage valuable views and realistic understanding which could inform your very non-public adventure.

Remember that achievement within the digital realm regularly includes innovation, staying energy, and the capacity to conform to changing situations, and these case research can serve as a supply of concept and steerage.

Troubleshooting and Problem Solving

In the dynamic world of on-line entrepreneurship, demanding conditions and setbacks are inevitable. This bankruptcy is dedicated to supporting you find out and triumph over commonplace issues that WordPress internet website online proprietors come across. By the stop of this monetary destroy, you could have acquired the expertise and abilties to navigate traumatic situations efficiently within the following key regions:

Common Challenges Faced via WordPress Website Owners: We will discover the identical antique hurdles and issues that website proprietors stumble upon. These also can encompass technical problems, declining net site site visitors, content fatigue, and further. Understanding the ones demanding conditions is the first step within the route of resolving them.

Solutions to Technical Issues: Technical machine faults can disrupt your internet website's capability and client experience. We will offer steerage on diagnosing and troubleshooting common technical issues, which encompass damaged hyperlinks, slow loading instances, and plugin conflicts.

Dealing with Setbacks and Staying Motivated: Maintaining motivation in the path of difficult instances is essential in your internet internet site on line's success. We will speak techniques for resilience, which include putting realistic expectations, looking for useful useful resource from the WordPress network, and locating inspiration to persevere.

Continuous Learning and Improvement: The digital landscape evolves unexpectedly, and staying informed is essential. We will discover strategies for non-forestall getting to know and professional development, in conjunction with retaining up with company tendencies and refining your abilities.

Troubleshooting and problem-solving are essential additives of coping with a WordPress website effectively. By gaining knowledge of the techniques and techniques presented in this bankruptcy, you may be higher prepared to navigate demanding situations and hold the resilience needed to thrive within the competitive on-line vicinity. Remember that each setback is an opportunity for boom and mastering, and your capacity to comply and triumph over boundaries is a hallmark of entrepreneurial fulfillment.

Wrapping Up and Looking Ahead

As we finish this complete guide to making money out of your WordPress net web page, it's far crucial to mirror for your adventure and chart a route for the destiny. In this very last bankruptcy, we are able to summarize key takeaways and offer steering on the subsequent key areas:

Summing Up Your WordPress Journey: We will revisit the crucial element requirements, techniques, and abilties you've got got obtained in the route of this e-book. Take a 2nd to reflect on how an prolonged manner you have were given are available your WordPress undertaking.

Setting New Goals and Directions: Success inside the virtual landscape is an ongoing pursuit. We will speak the significance of setting new dreams and evolving your website to fulfill converting developments and target market goals. Consider how you may bring together upon your present achievement.